Pensoso più d'altrui che di se stesso.

NICCOLÒ MACHIAVELLI

The Prince

Translation, Introduction and Notes
by Leo Paul S. de Alvarez

WAVELAND
PRESS, INC.

Long Grove, Illinois

For information about this book, contact:
Waveland Press, Inc.
4180 IL Route 83, Suite 101
Long Grove, IL 60047-9580
(847) 634-0081
info@waveland.com
www.waveland.com

Cover: *The cover picture is that of Michelangelo's idealized head of Lorenzo de' Medici, Duke of Urbino (to whom* The Prince *is dedicated), from the Chapel of the Medici, Church of San Lorenzo, Florence.*

Photograph: *Scala, Editorial Photocolor Archives.*

Printed in the United States of America

22   21   20

TABLE OF CONTENTS

MAPS

ACKNOWLEDGMENTS

I wish first to acknowledge my debt to Professor George Anastaplo of Rosary College and the University of Chicago. His seminars on Machiavelli at the University of Dallas and his continued suggestions have informed my understanding of specific passages in *The Prince*. I am also grateful for his encouragement and advice, which, since they come from a most prudent and courageous man, have always proved useful.

I also wish to thank Professor Harvey C. Mansfield, Jr., of Harvard University, and Professor Dain Trafton of Rockford College, whose suggestions were the cause of my rethinking and revising parts of the translation and of the introduction.

The deficiencies of the translation are, of course, entirely my responsibility.

My wife, Helen, has shared to a considerable degree in this work. Every aspect was discussed with her, from questions of grammar and style to the difficulties of interpreting certain passages. She also provided the translation of the Latin headings.

I am also grateful to the administrative assistants of the Politics Department of the University of Dallas, Mrs. Phyllis Eidelberg, Mrs. Wendy Hook, Mrs. Penny Van Sandt, and especially Miss Mary Zingleman and Mrs. Madeleine Myers, who all suffered through various revisions. Mrs. Myers prepared the Index of Proper Names.

I owe special thanks to Cecelia Brandon Schmitt who prepared the maps.

My colleagues, Professors John E. Alvis and Thomas G. West, kindly consented to read drafts of the translation and gave timely and helpful advice.

Finally, I wish to thank the students of my classes and seminars at the University of Dallas, in Rome and in Irving, on whom this translation was first tested, and whose questions and comments sharpened my study and understanding of *The Prince*.

Leo Paul S. de Alvarez

Irving, Texas
October, 1979

INTRODUCTION

This translation was begun as an exercise while I was teaching in Rome in 1972 for the University of Dallas. The course taught, which was officially called "Western Civilization," was in truth one on Thucydides and Machiavelli. Thus my first direct look at the remaining monuments of the greatness and power of Rome became at the same time an exploration of the works of the Greek general and the Florentine Secretary of State. Since students over the years have found the translation helpful, I have been persuaded to make it available generally as an alternative to the many translations of *The Prince* which have now been published. The difference between this translation and those of others will readily be noticed. The principal difference is that this translation attempts to be literal, in order to preserve the remarkable precision of Machiavelli's speech. I have tried, for example, to translate certain key terms consistently throughout — such as, for example, *acquistare* (to acquire), *arme* (arms), *ordinare* (to order) and *ordini* (orders), and, especially, *stato* (state) and *virtù* (virtue). The failure of most translations so to translate such terms is due, principally, to misleading assumptions about the plan and purpose of Machiavelli's work;[1] but it is also because of the desire to present a smoothly idiomatic English style, for a consistent translation will result in awkwardnesses which tempt one either to restructure the sentences completely, or, at worst, attempt paraphrases. But the question might be raised as to whether this is due to a prejudice on our part. We seem to expect that an author should write in a manner acceptable to our understanding, but the purpose of the awkwardnesses in an author such as Machiavelli is to point to difficulties which require a new way of thinking. Machiavelli himself says that he is the discoverer of a new land, the inventor of a new understanding of things,[2] and we cannot expect that his language should remain within the confines of the conventionally acceptable. Why then should one, in translating him, reduce or homogenize his language?

The modern reader should be warned that *The Prince* is not meant to be read either casually or quickly. Machiavelli demands an attentive reader who will ask questions of him, and like all good authors he provides the means whereby such a reader may discover the answers to the questions which must and should be asked. Among the reasons why this translation attempts to preserve the difficulties and ambiguities of the text is that Machiavelli is providing a puzzle which must be carefully and patiently worked through, and only those so willing to work will see what it is he has "with great diligence long reflected upon and examined." In other words, Machiavelli intends that the reader be caught up in the web of his discourse, and he does this by fascinating his reader with difficulties.

I.

I shall show the precision of Machiavelli, and the need, therefore, to translate consistently, by a discussion of two of his most important words, *stato* and *virtù*.[3] These two words are used in a way so strikingly new that they will serve to illustrate that new understanding mentioned above. *Lo stato* has been translated variously as station, dominion, rule, government, composition, position, reign, power and territory. One would indeed never know from the translations alone that Machiavelli has used the same word in all these instances. *Virtù* has also suffered from the inventiveness of the translators. It has been variously translated as valor, strength, courage, talent, ingenuity, strategy, efficacy, efficiency, quality, resource, capability, ability, character.

The difficulty with Machiavelli's use of *lo stato* can be seen most clearly when he speaks in Chapter III of the Romans who did not permit the Achaeans or the Aetolians to increase any state *(alcuno stato)* in Greece; nor would they consent that Antiochus "hold any state *(alcuno stato)* in that province." Thus one's "state" may increase or decrease in the same province; and there may be several who hold some "state" in the same province as, for example, the Achaeans, Aetolians, Antiochus and the Romans all held some "state" in Greece.

In Edward Dacres's 1640 translation, the word "state" is used throughout this particular passage. Mark Musa, however, translates *lo stato* first as "territory" and then as "authority." T. G. Bergin speaks of "holdings"; Allan H. Gilbert of "influence" and "importance"; the Modern Library edition first says "territory," and then, "the state." In the more recent translations, those of James B. Atkinson and Robert M. Adams, the same difficulty is encountered. Atkinson, for example, first uses the term "state" thus: "They (the Romans) never permitted the Achaeans or the Aetolians to expand their state." But the subsequent part of the sentence he renders as: "nor could the power Antiochus had make them agree to his holding any land in the region," where Machiavelli says "any state in that province." Adams's translation is even less literal; he uses "authority," "foothold," and "territory," for "state" and "province."[4]

Machiavelli's peculiar usage may be further seen from the following passages. In Chapter X, the question is asked as to whether "a prince has such state that if he finds himself in need, he can himself stand up by his own means . . ." Again, the translations vary: power, force, resources, position, strength, are substituted. In Chapter XI, the ancient orders of religion are said to keep ecclesiastical princes "in state," where one would today expect "in power." Similarly, in Chapter XX, some princes are said to have gained to themselves "those who were suspect at the beginning of their state," where one would expect something like the beginning of their rule or reign. However, in Chapter XII, the mercenaries are said to be "without state" and therefore dependent on "their own industry." This sentence is usually interpreted to mean that the mercenaries were without land, a territory, or country. And in Chapter XXIV, Philip of Macedon is said not to have had "much state," which is then also usually translated in terms of possessing territory.

In these examples, *lo stato* appears to have meanings too diverse to be encompassed in one word, such as "the state." It appears to refer to territory, to rule or reign, to power, to status and authority. What we mean today by "the state," is, of course, a body politic which possesses above all the characteristic of sovereignty, but Machiavelli seems seldom to use *lo stato* with that particular meaning. For *lo stato* in Machiavelli is not an acting body; it is instead acquired, seized, held, maintained, conserved, ruined, taken away and lost; it is ordered and disordered, created, established, ruled and increased. Only in two instances is it suggested that the state may act rather than be acted upon. In Chapter XXI, it is said that no state ought ever to believe "that it is always able to pick a part safely." And in Chapter IV, it is said of the state of Asia that it would have been reasonable for that state to have rebelled against the successors of Alexander the Great.[5]

We may, I believe, begin to grasp what Machiavelli means by *lo stato,* by considering the significance of his making touch the most important sense; that is, the sense which alone can provide certain knowledge. In Chapter XVIII, he observes that "men universally judge more by the eyes than by the hands; because it is given to everyone that they see, but to few that they can touch." The sense of sight is misleading, for appearances are misleading. One is reminded of Rousseau's Emile who has to learn not to trust his sense of sight. Emile is shown that a stick which appears bent, when viewed through water, still feels straight when he touches it.[6] The raising of the importance of the sense of touch as the most certain, if not the noblest sense, is one of the fundamental differences which divides the moderns from the ancients.

"Everyone," says Machiavelli, "sees what you seem to be, but few touch what you are, and those few will not dare to oppose themselves to the opinions of the many . . ." Appearances deceive, and few can touch the truth behind the appearances; but the many live by appearances and will not believe anything other. The few who do understand are helpless politically, for the few will "not dare to oppose themselves to the opinions of many who have the majesty of the state defending them."

But understanding, going beyond the appearances, is obviously necessary for the prince. Understanding is not as politically helpless as Machiavelli would seem to have us believe, for the prince, who does understand, must be able to manipulate appearances or opinions of the many, but only he can do so. He grasps or acquires the state, and in so doing goes beyond the opinion of the people to the "effectual truth" of things. He lives not by appearances but by what he can touch, but since the people do live by appearances, he is forced to manipulate these appearances to his own purposes: "Let a prince then win and maintain the state — the means will always be judged honorable and will be praised by everyone; for the vulgar are always taken by the appearance and with the outcome of a thing; and in this world there is no one but the vulgar . . ."

If appearances are deceiving, if we cannot trust what we see, then we must use a different way of knowing the truth of things. But to go beyond appearances demands a method; that is, we must have a way of protecting ourselves against the deceptions of sight. We must first begin to understand in what ways one can be misled, and in what ways one can touch and therefore have certain knowledge.

The need to establish method means that man, through his reason, must impose an order where there is none. He is forced, by means of his thought, to make his own order, his own way or mode of action, *in acque e terre incognite*,[7] to come to know things. Reason is methodic science; man thinks of how he is to approach things first before he can begin to grasp them. He cannot begin with appearances — that is, try to understand by seeing.

A further consequence of making touch the primary sense is to be seen most clearly in Chapter VI. After he names the four great founders, Moses, Cyrus, Romulus and Theseus, he observes that: "in examining their actions and life, one sees that fortune provided them with nothing other than the occasion which gave them the matter into which they could introduce whatever form they pleased . . ." In sum, the will becomes primary. The most excellent kind of man, the founder of new orders and modes is characterized by possessing such virtue of mind (the body is not mentioned here, and Machiavelli never speaks of the soul in *The Prince*)[8] that he can introduce whatever form he pleases or wills when the proper matter or occasion is given him. Nature herself does not provide the form; the form must be given, or perhaps imposed, by the mind of man.

We have seen that the state is different from a province. We may now, I believe, understand the distinction. The province is the land and its inhabitants which, like all natural things, remains ever the same (See *Discourses,* III.43: "That men, born in a province, maintain in all times almost the same nature.") The country or province is the matter into which a virtuous prince, if his modes are suitable, introduces whatever form or order he pleases.

We need now to make a brief digression to consider that well-known Machiavellian phrase, "modes and orders." We suggest that one should understand the state as the extent to which the will of the prince is imposed upon the matter which is given him. The visible manifestations of that will are the "orders" which he establishes. I believe it to be significant that in Chapter VI he speaks of "orders and modes," and not of "modes and orders" as he does in the Preface to Book I of the *Discourses*. The order or the form is the construct of the mind of some excellent man. But he must have the proper matter or the occasion; otherwise he will be unable to actualize the form he wills. Whether or not he will have the occasion is something which would seem to be given by fortune. Matter and fortune are thus linked together; we can say that nature and fortune are perhaps one and the same. One of the great questions, and it is perhaps *the* great question, which Machiavelli raises in *The Prince*, is the extent to which fortune may be mastered. Now what Machiavelli seems to mean by "modes" is, for example, whether a prince is circumspect or impetuous (Ch. XXV), cruel or full of pity (Ch. XVII). The matter, which is the people, requires, at times, that a prince be extraordinarily cruel; at times, that he show pity; at times, that he be impetuous, at others that he be circumspect or cautious. And when, Machiavelli concludes, the times and the prince's modes do not coincide, he is unhappy — that is, fails to introduce his orders. If a prince were then able to change his modes with the times he would always be happy, always master Fortuna (Ch. XXV). Machiavelli seems to say that it is humanly impossible so to change one's modes, but is it simply impossible? A prince's modes are, we may say, his adaptation to circumstances, to the world of appearances; if he could always adapt himself quickly to circumstances, his orders would never fail.

To return: since the state is the construct of the mind and the will, it may increase or decrease in the same province; and it is possible for several to have a state in the same province. The state is the realization in act of the will of someone. It indicates the extent to which one's will is introduced or imposed. Machiavelli is exact in the use of the word. We should note that Machiavelli always speaks of the state as being someone's; it seems to have no being apart from the capacity of someone to act. It is thus the greatest manifestation of the *virtù* or excellence of a man.

Machiavelli has indeed abandoned ancient orders and modes. The *polis,* we remind ourselves, was said by Aristotle to be the association for the complete life of man. The *polis* is by nature; it is not simply a man-made thing. It has definite limits and a definite order which serve as guides for men to follow. Nature herself presents men with an order capable of being understood and followed. But the state is whatever is willed by the prince — it is whatever he pleases. No natural order guides that pleasure; there is only the matter which may either be more or less resistant to what is willed. The state is limitless; its only limits are due to circumstance and therefore accident; due, as Machiavelli says, to fortune.

The state, then, is certainly not a territory, and it is more than rule, power, dominion or government. It is the ordering of inchoate nature into a human form. It is entirely an artificial construct, dependent upon man's capacity to invent and to manipulate things. By resisting the temptation to make Machiavelli more understandable, we come to understand more clearly what the state is; that original understanding still remains, for the state has been thought of in the nineteenth and twentieth centuries in terms primarily of the will and not of nature.[9]

Two words which must be linked to this understanding of the state are: *il principato,* the principate; and *l'imperio,* the imperium. By translating *il principato* as "the principate," one places emphasis upon the will of him who rules, and not upon *that* which he rules, the principality — which is what the latter term tends to connote to us today.

Similarly, to translate *l'imperio* as "the empire," tends to put the emphasis upon that which is ruled, rather than upon him who commands. It is the imperium of the prince, the power to command, which is of importance, and not the peoples or territories which he rules.

II.

The difficulties with Machiavelli's use of *virtù* emerge most clearly in Chapter VIII, when, in speaking of Agathocles the Sicilian, he observes that he attained to the principate by means of great *virtù* of mind and body, and not therefore by fortune. But he subsequently adds: "one cannot call it *virtù* to kill his fellow citizens, to betray his friends, to be without faith, without pity, without religion; which modes enabled him to acquire imperium, but not glory." Immediately afterwards, however, he speaks again of the *virtù* of Agathocles, and the greatness of his mind. He adds, in the sequel, the observation that he does not see why Agathocles "should have to be judged inferior to any of the most excellent captains;" and he finally concludes that Agathocles's "brutal cruelty and inhumanity" prevent him from being ranked "among the most excellent celebrated men."

In this passage, Machiavelli exposes the difficulty of the term *virtù*. One may speak of *virtù* in the older sense which is connected with manliness, of having strength of body and mind, and especially of being able to acquire and keep a state. *Virtù* here is an excellence which has little connection with what we today would understand by morality. In this sense Agathocles possesses such greatness of mind and body, that one may speak of his *virtù*.

But, as Machiavelli says, one cannot call it *virtù* when one kills his fellow-citizens. Here *virtù* is understood to be acting in accordance with justice and the good. It is to be virtuous in the ordinarily accepted sense which refers to the goodness and justice of the disposition of a man's soul and of his actions. In this sense, Agathocles certainly cannot be called virtuous. One must point out that the most excellent celebrated men are noted for their justice and goodness, by which is meant Moses, and also Cyrus, Romulus and Theseus.

That Machiavelli understood the difference in these two notions of *virtù* is obvious. But he deliberately uses only one word to denote both greatness of mind and body, and that which is

morally righteous. Why does he use the same word? It is that difficulty which leads the translators to speak of the ingenuity, or
valor, or prowess, of Agathocles, which then results in, for example, Mark Musa making Machiavelli say, "Yet it cannot be called
ingenuity to kill one's fellow-citizens, etc.," when it precisely can
be called ingenuity, but not virtue. The simple conclusion is that
Machiavelli deliberately wishes to confuse the two meanings.
Since he knew that one cannot call it *virtù* to be inhumanly cruel,
why does he persist in speaking of men who commit such acts as
virtuous? But before we ask why he wished to confuse, there is yet
a third meaning of *virtù* that we must consider.

In Chapter XII, mercenaries are described as neither fearing
God nor possessing faith in men. The argument on the inutility of
mercenary arms, the details of which I must omit here, concludes
in the necessity of a prince arming himself with his own arms and
in his own mode. To do so, however, as is explained in Chapters
IX, X and XX, he must gain the people's support, for to have
one's own arms is necessarily to arm the people. But if
mercenaries do not fear God, must we not assume that an armed
people should fear God?

The answer to this question is given by Machiavelli in the
Discourses.[10] The Romans were religious. A comparison of the
titles of Chapters 11 to 13 in Book I of the *Discourses,* with the
corresponding titles of the chapters in *The Prince* is revealing.
Chapter XI of *The Prince* is: "Of Ecclesiastical Principates;"
Chapter 11 of Book I of the *Discourses* is, "Of the Religion of the
Romans." The Church and the pagan religion are once more con-
fronted one with another. Chapter XII of *The Prince* is, "How
Many Kinds of Militia There Are and About Mercenary Soldiers," and it is concerned principally with the failure of Italy to be
armed and free and not dependent on the arms of others and there-
fore on fortune. The title of Chapter 12, Book I, of the *Discourses* is,
"Of How Much Importance It Is to Take Account of Religion, and
How Italy, By Being in Lack of It Because of the Church, Is

Ruined." The Roman religion is a true religion because it helps to arm and defend the people. The religion represented by the Church, which may not necessarily be the Christian religion, is no religion. Indeed, the Church has made Italy lack religion, and has left her disarmed and ruined. The chapter in *The Prince* on mercenaries corresponds to the chapter on the Church in the *Discourses*. The Church is the cause of Italy's dependence on mercenary arms, "which do not fear God, nor do they have faith in men." Italy sins by not having religion; she is in need of a redeemer; but, as he says in Chapter XII, the sins are not those of which Savonarola spoke, and neither is the redeemer.

The third meaning of *virtù* is, then, the religion which binds men together into a city, and which will, in adversity, with faith defend it (Ch. XIII). *Virtù* here denotes the civic religion, the religion which makes the people obstinate in the defense of their city.

By referring to the city and not to the state, I mean to indicate that Machiavelli considers such *virtù* to be peculiarly republican. The prince, as he acknowledges in the *Discourses,* has less need of religion than a republic (I.11, penult. para.).

The use of one word for three quite distinct meanings leads, as I have said, to confusion. But that confusion has the effect of casting doubt, especially upon the understanding of *virtù* as justice and righteousness. We are left with a doubt as to whether men like Cesare Borgia are virtuous or vicious, and it is not surprising that Machiavelli's praise of Cesare has misled a few scholars into an attempt to show that the historical Cesare did measure up to what Machiavelli says is required of a founder of a fatherland. The confusion leads to moral ambiguity; moral ambiguity leads to a willingness to re-examine present orders and modes (see *Discourses,* III.8). Only by permitting the confusion to remain will we be able to detect Machiavelli's scheme. That is, only by permitting *virtù* to remain virtue can we experience that effect which Machiavelli has so carefully, so cunningly, planned. The purpose of Chapters XV to XVIII of *The Prince* is surely to undermine what we believe ought to be blamed or praised, held to be a virtue or a vice. As he observes at the end of Chapter XV, "if one will consider all things well, he will find something which will seem *virtù* itself, and his conforming to it would be his ruin; and something other which will seem vice itself, and his conforming to it would succeed in his security and well-being." Nowhere is this ambiguity of virtue made more emphatic than at the conclusion of the story of Oliverotto da Fermo in Chapter VIII, who was, Machiavelli says, captured by Cesare Borgia and "together with Vitellozo who had been his teacher in virtue and wickednesses, strangled."

My purpose in working out how Machiavelli uses *stato* and *virtù* was to establish the point that he is an exceedingly careful and precise writer, and that if he therefore chooses to use words in ways which seem to us to be strange, we should remind ourselves that there must be a reason for such strangeness, and that he means for us to think of what that reason might be. Machiavelli can say, as Rousseau subsequently did, "I warn the reader . . . that I do not know the art of being clear for him who will not be attentive" (*Social Contract,* II.1). I have therefore, to repeat, attempted to translate the key Machiavellian terms as consistently as possible throughout.

III.

One other benefit which, as I have discovered, a literal translation gives, is that it permits the text itself to reveal subtleties which not only disappear in less literal translations, but are, as it were, entirely obliterated. For, as Machiavelli says (Ch. III), *The Prince* is a woven piece of work and, like a beautiful carpet, it has very subtle patterns.

I shall attempt further to demonstrate the usefulness of a literal translation by an analysis of the Epistle Dedicatory which will, I believe, show why one must preserve the sometimes convoluted structure of Machiavelli's sentences, for the very form in which he presents his thought is necessary for the coming to light of that thought. I shall then give three examples of what I have called subtle patterns in the weave of his thought.

The Prince is addressed to the Magnificent Lorenzo de' Medici. It is addressed to one man, a prince, in this case the Duke of Urbino. The name reminds us of the famed Lorenzo the Magnificent, so well-known for his patronage of the arts and learning. The Lorenzo whom Machiavelli addresses is however the grandson of his namesake and the nephew of Pope Leo X, Giovanni de' Medici. This Lorenzo came to his title through the efforts of other members of his House. He did not himself earn his title by his own deeds.

The use of Latin in the epistolary address is conventional. The immediate impression is that this is the courtier's conventional supplication of a prince. Instead of continuing in Latin, however, Machiavelli somewhat surprises us by using the vulgar tongue. It is the first indication of the character of the book, which combines the conventional with the novel.

The first sentence of the Dedication begins with what is usual, what is done most of the time by most men when they desire to acquire favor before a prince. He begins with men who desire to acquire something, and one might suspect that this is the usual condition of most men. To acquire favor, men bring to the prince either what seems to them to be delightful or what they see pleases him. In either case, what is brought enhances the magnificence of the prince. The gifts brought display the prince's sumptuousness, what they signify above all is that he has no needs; he can be concerned with the beautiful and not with the useful.

A reversal occurs in the second part of the first sentence. In the first clause, we are told of the many who approach the one, the prince, and of the usual gifts they bring. In the second clause, the one prince becomes the many princes. Machiavelli accomplishes this sudden turn at the expense of the correct use of number; he thus calls attention to the forced grammatical change. The singular prince is now the plural "they," the many princes, and in the next sentence he emphatically speaks of "I" — the one who now approaches the many. This "I" is a desiring I. In that respect he is equal to the many who seek the favor of the prince. He too is in need, but unlike the many who come to the one, he is one who comes to the many. He is therefore to be distinguished in some way from the many. The prince, on the other hand, is now the many. Are the princes then in some fundamental respect the same as the many?

Machiavelli offers his "little" book as a testimony of his desire to be in fealty to Lorenzo the Magnificent. He claims to have been able to distill his knowledge of the actions of great men into "a little volume;" that is, he has made it easy for others, as he subsequently says, to understand what has taken him years of hardship to come to know and to understand. It is apparently hard to come to know, while someone may make it easy for another to understand. The actions of great men cannot be known and understood without "experience of modern things," and "the continuous reading of ancient [things]." Present deeds need to be illumined by ancient ones.

The book is the best of Machiavelli's "equipment" — he uses the term *suppellettile,* which has as its technical meaning, "military equipment." Machiavelli's "equipment" must of course be contrasted with the "ornaments" which the many and the princes alike believe to be worthy of "greatness." What Machiavelli brings is not the usual gift which is thought proper to give to greatness; instead his gift to magnificence, as is implied in the word "equipment," is that which is useful. Machiavelli implies, therefore, that Lorenzo the Magnificent is in need — in need of the useful thing which Machiavelli alone can provide; he is perhaps then as needy in his own way as is Machiavelli. Is magnificence therefore a sham? Men, it would seem, are in need, whether they be high or low, fortunate or unfortunate, and their true condition is one of desiring. Magnificence, as we have said, is a display of unnecessitous beauty; the magnificent man's ostentation proclaims that he is, like a god, completely self-sufficient. But is anyone, in truth, self-sufficient? Machiavelli, at the beginning of his treatise, seems to indicate otherwise.

The work, although useful, is judged by Machiavelli himself as unworthy of the presence of magnificence. The incompatibility of these two qualities one with another is thus stated again. Machiavelli's judgment is here in accord with that of the many. But he then makes clear in the subsequent sentence that the "pompous and magnificent" and "artifices and extrinsic ornaments" are things which ought to be avoided by those who would know and understand. Not the magnificence but the humanity of the Duke will, however, lead him to accept the gift of the work. Machiavelli does not say that the Duke will come to understand all that he, Machiavelli, has come to understand. What is said instead is that the Duke will take into account the fact that one cannot expect from Machiavelli a greater gift. Humanity would seem to consist in not expecting too much of those who are less endowed or blessed than oneself. All that Lorenzo will perhaps learn is that Machiavelli truly desires to be of service to the Duke.[11] That is all Lorenzo needs to get and perhaps can get from the book. We must expect, therefore, that Machiavelli must somehow prove in the book that he is indeed loyal to Lorenzo and not dangerous to him. Lorenzo is in need of the understanding in Machiavelli's book, but it is a need which cannot be met by Lorenzo's reading of the book. What Lorenzo will learn from the book is the loyalty of Machiavelli, which will then induce the former to accept the latter's gift of himself. The final paragraph states that Lorenzo by the diligent reading of the book will learn of Machiavelli's "extreme desire" that he, Lorenzo, "come to that greatness which fortune and his other qualities promise."

However, the prince, we are told, knows something which others cannot know. He knows of the low places, of the nature of the people, in a way which others who are not princes cannot. The prince does not know well the nature of princes; that is, he does not know himself. How seriously we are to take these remarks is perhaps indicated subsequently, when, as we have seen, Machiavelli suggests the limits of what Lorenzo can learn from the book. Moreover, in Chapter XIV he points out that the prince must come to know the nature of *all* the sites and places. It does seem odd that the man on high should know principally of low things; the people know the high things better than do the princes. Is there a hint here of Machiavelli's democratic preferences?

But let us note again what it is that Machiavelli says the prince lacks and which therefore must be supplied. Machiavelli claims to be able to supply knowledge and understanding of the nature of princes or the actions of great men. But what are great actions but rule over human beings? What Machiavelli says, and with a certain insulting boldness, is that Lorenzo does not know the actions of great men. Not to know the actions of great men is the same as not knowing how princes act. But not to know how princes act is not to know how to rule. Machiavelli seems confident that Lorenzo will not draw this inference, and will not therefore recognize the very great insult.

The Duke is promised greatness by fortune;[12] Machiavelli, in contrast, suffers under a "great and continuous malignity of fortune." Is this the principal difference between the two?[13] One wonders if an "extraordinary and extreme" malignity of fortune would have sufficed to keep Machiavelli down. What is perhaps important is the continuousness of the malignity of fortune. But how can one promise that fortune will continue to favor Lorenzo? We learn later that it is not fortune but virtue which makes secure the modes and orders of a prince. Virtue is that alone by which Fortuna can be mastered, and Machiavelli is silent upon Lorenzo's virtue, that is, silent upon his capacity to stand up to fortune.

The Epistle Dedicatory of *The Prince* is thus marked by a subtle but nonetheless effective derogation of Lorenzo de' Medici. It becomes evident that the work cannot possibly be addressed to Lorenzo; for, as is said in Chapter XV, it is Machiavelli's "intention to write a useful thing for him who understands." We are led to realize that *The Prince* is a supremely ironic work; and we must especially begin to wonder about its "Italian" and "patriotic" aspect, since it is to the House of the Medici that the exhortation is made to liberate and redeem Italy — a House which is unequal to the task, for its power is dependent on fortune and does not arise from its own virtue.

We have also noted certain themes in the Epistle Dedicatory — the neediness of human beings; the desire to acquire as the principal human passion; and the replacement of the magnificent or the beautiful by the useful. Machiavelli has embarked us upon the new or modern enterprise of conquering nature for the sake of the relief of man's estate. Not the enterprise of Italy but that of mankind is what Machiavelli newly undertakes.

A brief perusal of other translations of the Epistle Dedicatory reveals, in the first place, a tendency to correct the grammar of the first sentence. Thus Adams, in the most recent translation, so renders the sentence that the tension in the implicit question of who is the one and who is the many dissolves into nothing. Nor, as far as I have seen, has anyone noticed that heightening of the difference between the magnificent or beautiful and the useful, introduced by the term *suppellettile*. One should include in the series of tensions carefully set up in the first paragraph, that between modern experience and ancient writings.

IV.

1.

Three examples will further illustrate the argument for the felicity of a literal text. In every translation I have consulted the

Machiavellian by-play on the difference between "power" and "greatness" in Chapters III, VII, and XI is completely lost. As a consequence, one loses a Machiavellian suggestion as to how one should understand the Church. To begin with, when Machiavelli first mentions the Romans in Chapter III, he uses the word "power" like an insistent drumbeat:

> The Romans, in the provinces they took, observed well these matters: they sent colonies, kept and provided for the less powerful without increasing their power, put down the powers, and never let powerful foreigners gain a reputation . . .

But when he speaks of the Church at the end of Chapter III, he speaks of "the greatness" of the Church and not of its power. Indeed, he seems to go out of his way to avoid speaking of the Church as powerful when it would seem natural to do so. That one has a natural inclination to use the word "powerful" in connection with the Church is indicated by the fact that every recent translation has succumbed to that inclination, particularly in that passage (in Chapter III) which reads:

> . . . Nor did he [the King of France] perceive that with this deliberation he weakened himself, removing his own friends and those who had been thrown into his lap from himself, and made the Church great, adding to the spiritual, which already gives her so much authority, so much of the temporal.

The temptation to add "power" to complete the thought — thus saying "spiritual power" and "temporal power" — is, as I said, almost irresistible; but it must be resisted. For Machiavelli refuses to speak of the Church's power until Chapter XI, when, with the pontificate of Leo X, he finally speaks of the pontiff, and not the Church, as powerful. The reason is clear. The pontiff has gained arms. (He does seem to speak once, but only indirectly, of the Church as powerful. He says that King Louis XII of France committed five errors in his invasion of Italy, the second of which is that "he increased the power of someone already powerful in Italy." We note, however, that he did not choose directly to connect "Church" and "power.") We learn from the first sentence of Chapter XI that the Church's greatness is due to her being "ancient," that is, to the people having become accustomed to her rule. Greatness seems to be equivalent to reputation, and it would then be dependent upon opinion. Greatness would therefore not have the certainty or solidity of power.[14] It can therefore be the gift of fortune and not of arms. When Machiavelli speaks of the ancient Roman virtue, he speaks not of greatness but of power. We notice, finally, that Machiavelli's last word on the Church is that one would wish her to be "great and venerated," but he is silent upon one's wishing her to be powerful.

To summarize: when the Church, through the pontiff, gains arms, then and only then is it correct to say that she is powerful.[15] Machiavelli anticipates a twentieth-century tyrant's question as to how many divisions the Pope has.

2.

Another of Machiavelli's intricate weavings has to do with his use of the word *condotta,* which is the contract that a city makes with a mercenary captain and his company of soldiers. Hence the term *condottieri* is used of the mercenaries. In Chapter XII, the chapter on mercenary arms, Machiavelli ends the chapter with a pun upon *condotta: "tanto che gli hanno condotta Italia stiava e vituperata"* — "such that they have conducted Italy into slavery and contempt." The reliance on the *condotta* (contract) with *condottieri* (mercenaries) *ha condotta* (has conducted) Italy into slavery.

Machiavelli also puns with the word in Chapter VII, where he recounts the adventures of Cesare Borgia. Cesare almost conducts *(condotta)* Italy into the hands of the Church. But it is not only Cesare who is a "conductor"; Pope Julius II is also a "conductor," for, as Machiavelli says (Chapter XXI), Julius conducts "with his impetuous motion, that which another pontiff, with all human prudence, would never have conducted."

The final use of *condotta* appears in Chapter XXVI, where God is said to have "conducted" extraordinary things. The Biblical references in this passage necessarily remind us that it was Moses who was the conductor of Israel to the Promised Land, and that Moses was, as Chapter VI says, "a mere executor of the things that were ordained by God." One realizes that God, Moses, and Cesare are all "conductors," that is, *condottieri,* and one sees more fully what is meant by saying that Italy's reliance upon "conductors" has enslaved her.[16]

3.

The final example I shall cite is Machiavelli's use of the term *rimettersi.* At the end of Chapter XIII, Machiavelli says: *"a quali ordini io al tutto mi rimetto."* I had great difficulty in capturing the nuances of this phrase. I discovered, however, that in Chapter XXIII, the last paragraph, Machiavelli also uses *rimettersi —* *"si gia a sorte non si rimettersi in uno solo che al tutto lo governarsi,"* which is easily translated as, "unless by chance he consigns himself to one who alone will wholly govern him." It would appear that as an unwise prince should give himself over completely to a prudent counselor, so Machiavelli gives himself over completely to the orders of great men. Thus I decided to translate the phrase at the end of Chapter XIII as: "to which orders, I, in all things, consign myself," with the echo of giving oneself up completely to what one believes in — as when one consigns one's soul to God.[17]

4.

I have mentioned these examples to indicate how only a literal translation is able to preserve something of these patterns. In none of the translations previously cited, for example, does one get the slightest hint of the playing with *condotta,* or with *grandezza* (greatness) and *potenzia* (power). And most of the translations fail to preserve significant repetitions of words, rarely used elsewhere in the text, such as, for example, the repetition of *precettore* (preceptor) in Chapters VI and XVIII; and they fail also to maintain the rhythm of his constant use of certain words such as *modo* (mode), *necessità* (necessity), *sangue* (blood), *materia* (matter), etc. The purpose of this translation is to enable the reader to make these discoveries for himself.

V.

The text followed in this translation is that of the edition by Francesco Flora and Carlo Cordié (Verona: Arnoldo Mondadori, 1968), and the paragraphing follows the one in that edition. I have of course consulted other translations, to which I certainly owe a debt.

The notes are chiefly meant for the student who usually is not acquainted with the names, events and places which Machiavelli mentions. The notes also explain the translation and indicate passages in other works, principally Machiavelli's, which may prove helpful in understanding the text.

Machiavelli tells us in Chapter XIV that the prince ought to undertake two kinds of exercise, one of works and the other of the intellect, the exercise of the body and that of the mind. The exercise of the body is the hunt, and it is an exercise in particulars. The exercise of the mind is the reading of histories and the imitation of the most excellent men, and it is an exercise in universals.

The Prince may also be said to give us two kinds of exercise — in the particulars of the events which took place in Italy from 1494 to 1513, and in those universals which lead us back to the deeds of the Romans and the writings of Xenophon. We must pay attention to both these orders of exercise if we are to begin to learn how to read Machiavelli. For in coming to know the things of Italy, we also come to know the universal human things.

Notes

1. A new understanding of Machiavelli requires a new translation. That new understanding has been provided by Leo Strauss's *Thoughts on Machiavelli* (Glencoe, Ill.: Free Press, 1958), which work can be said to have rediscovered Machiavelli. The seeming inconsistencies and contradictions that for so long had puzzled scholars were shown by Professor Strauss to have been only the surface of an exceedingly well-thought-out argument. When the assumptions that have guided former readers of Machiavelli have been shown to be misleading, then one cannot but come to suspect the translations produced under such guidance. I will not go into the scholarly controversies over the interpretation of the work of Machiavelli. But see Willmoore Kendall's review of *Thoughts on Machiavelli* in *Contra Mundum* (New Rochelle, N.Y.: Arlington House, 1971), pp. 449-456. This review was first published in *The Philosophical Review*, LXII (April, 1966). See also Harvey C. Mansfield, Jr., and J. G. A. Pocock, "An Exchange on Strauss's Machiavelli," in *Political Theory*, III (Nov., 1975), pp. 372-405.

2. *Discourses on the First Ten Books of Titus Livy*, I. Preface.

3. A detailed study of Machiavelli's use of the term *lo stato* has been made by J. H. Hexter, "*Il Principe* and *lo stato*," *Studies in the Renaissance* IV (1956), pp. 113-138. Hexter counts 114 occurrences of *lo stato* or its plural form in a work 15,000 words long. My own count is 116, including one occurrence in the Epistle Dedicatory. The majority of occurrences of the term is to be found in Chapters III, IV, XIX and XX.

Mark Musa, in his translation of *The Prince* (New York: St. Martin's Press, 1964), pp. x-xv, counts 59 occurrences of *virtù*, three of *virtuoso* (Chapters, VI, VII, XXVI), and one of *virtuosissimamente* (Ch. XII). He does not however count the one time it occurs in a chapter heading (Ch. VI).

Musa also counts 51 occurrences of *fortuna*; 17 in connection with *virtù*. My own count indicates 52 instances of *fortuna* and one of *fortunata*.

4. The Edward Dacres translation is to be found in *Machiavelli,* with an introduction by Henry Cust (London: D. Nutt, 1905), The Tudor Translations, I.

Thomas G. Bergin's translation is published in the Crofts Classics series (N.Y.: Appleton-Century Crofts, 1947).

Allan H. Gilbert's translation is in his edition of Machiavelli, *The Chief Works* (Durham, N.C.: Duke University Press, 1965) I.

James B. Atkinson's translation is published by the Library of Liberal Arts (Indianapolis: Bobbs-Merrill, 1976).

Robert M. Adams's translation is a Norton Critical Edition (N.Y.: N. W. Norton & Co., 1977).

5. I am indebted to Hexter who saved me labor in working out Machiavelli's usage. See n. 3, above.

6. *Emile* (New York: Basic Books, 1979) Introduction, Translation, and Notes by Allan Bloom, pp. 205-207 (Book III) and pp. 140, 143 (Book II).

7. *in unknown waters and lands* — *Discourses,* I. Preface.

8. See the Epistle Dedicatory, n. 8, below.

9. It is generally acknowledged that our word "the state," is ultimately derived from Machiavelli's use of *lo stato.* See, for instance, "State," *Encyclopedia Americana,* 1924 ed.; "State," *International Encyclopedia of the Social Sciences,* 1968 ed.; and "The State," *The New Encyclopedia Britannica: Macropaedia,* 1979 ed. If, as Prof. Leo Strauss says, Machiavelli deserves the honor of being the originator of modern political philosophy, then central to modern political philosophy is the question of the state. Leo Strauss, *The Political Philosophy of Hobbes,* translated from the German by Elsa M. Sinclair (Chicago: University of Chicago Press, Phoenix ed., 1963), p. xv.

See also Bernard Bosanquet, *The Philosophical Theory of the State* (London: Macmillan and Co., 1930), pp. lvi-lvii, and especially Chapters V and X. Bosanquet reviews the understanding of the state as will.

10. Indeed one may say generally that there appears to be a correspondence between certain chapters of *The Prince* and the *Discourses,* so much so that one must conclude that Machiavelli intends us to compare these chapters one with another. It should of course be noted that the relationship between these two works is obscure and difficult, but both works claim to present all that Machiavelli has come to know and understand. See Strauss, *Thoughts on Machiavelli,* Ch. I. See Harvey C. Mansfield, Jr., *Machiavelli's New Modes and Orders* (Ithaca: Cornell University Press, 1979), p. 9.

11. Compare Ch. XXII, below.

12. On the ambiguity of "greatness," see the discussion in section IV of this Introduction.

13. See the Epistle Dedicatory, n. 10, below.

14. The Epistle Dedicatory speaks of Machiavelli's "knowledge of the actions of great men;" now the greatest examples of such great men are Moses, Cyrus, Romulus and Theseus. But see Ch. VI, n. 3, below, on the possibility of others who while not "great" may yet be of more significance.

15. See Ch. III, n. 23, below.

16. See Ch. VII, n. 13, and Ch. XII, n. 23, below.

17. See Ch. XIII, n. 15, below.

The Italian States of the Late 15th Century

C. Brandon Schmitt 1979

NICCOLÒ MACHIAVELLI TO THE
MAGNIFICENT LORENZO MEDICI *

Usually, in most cases,[1] those who desire to acquire grace before
a Prince,[2] make themselves come up to meet him with those
things that among them are held most dear, or that they see
delight him the most; whence one sees them many times being
presented with horses, arms, gold cloths, precious stones, and
similar ornaments worthy of their greatness.[3] I desiring, then, to
offer myself to Your Magnificence with some testimony of my
fealty to that [Magnificence],[4] have not found among my
equipment,[5] anything that I hold most dear or so esteem as the
knowledge of the actions of great men, learned by me through
long experience of modern things and the continuous readings of
ancient [things];[6] which I, having with great diligence long
reflected upon and examined, and now reduced into a little
volume, send to Your Magnificence.

And although I judge this work unworthy of the presence of
[His Magnificence], yet I very much trust that it should be
accepted through his humanity, considering how there cannot be
had a greater gift from me than to give to one the faculty of being
able in a very short time to understand all that I, in so many years

Nicolaus Maclevellus ad Magnificium Laurentiam Medicem

1

and in so many of my hardships and dangers, have come to know and to understand. This work I have not ornamented either with the fullness of extended clauses, or with pompous and magnificent words, or with whatever artifices or extrinsic ornaments with which they[7] most usually describe and ornament their things; because I have wished that it not be honored for any of these things but that only the variety of the matter and the weight of the theme give it grace. Nor do I wish it to be thought presumptuous if a man of low and mean state dares to discuss and to regulate the government of princes; for, just as those who sketch the countryside place themselves below in the plain to consider the nature of mountains and high places, and in order to consider the low places they put themselves high on the mountains, similarly, to come to know well the nature of the people one needs to be a prince and to know well that of princes one needs to be of the people.

Take, then, Your Magnificence, this little gift with that spirit[8] with which I send it; which, if it is by [His Magnificence] with care diligently considered and read, he will come to know in it my extreme desire, that He[9] come to know that greatness which fortune and his other qualities promise. And if Your Magnificence from the peak of his height will turn his eyes at some time to these low places, he will know how undeservedly I bear a great and continuous malignity of fortune.[10]

Notes

1. *sogliono (solere)* — Machiavelli not only begins with "they usually," he redundantly adds, *il più delle volte,* "most times" or "in most cases," to emphasize that he is not going to do as men in similar situations usually do. It is evidently important to understand what is usually done, what is done in most cases. For a discussion of the Epistle Dedicatory, see the Introduction.

2. *acquistare grazia appresso uno Principe* — That is, to acquire a pleasing and attractive aspect in the eyes of the Prince.

3. One should notice that the many approach the one Prince in the first part of the sentence; but in the second part of the sentence the one Prince becomes the many princes who delight in the things that the many suitors bring, and the author becomes a *one* (unlike the many who usually give gifts) — thus, the author becomes like the Prince. As it is well-known, Machiavelli sometimes changes from the singular to the plural, and vice-versa, seemingly without concerning himself with correct grammar. See Mark Musa, translator and editor, *The Prince* (New York: St. Martin's Press, 1964), pp. xv-xvi, 3 (n.2). Hereafter cited as Musa.

4. *della servitù mia verso di quella* — Machiavelli wishes to give testimony of his homage or fealty *(servitù)* to *that (quella)*, that is, to Lorenzo's Magnificence and not to the man himself. My use of the term "fealty" is, I believe, in keeping with the image of feudal ceremony evoked by the opening sentence.

The subtle irony of the Epistle Dedicatory cannot be reproduced in translation. Thus it is to the Magnificence of Yours *(Magnificentia Vostra)* that he sends his little volume. And, at the beginning of the second paragraph, it is to that Magnificence that he compares his book. In contrast to the beauty of the gifts usually presented, Machiavelli has "equipment" [*suppellettile*] (see n. 5 below). One is reminded of Thucydides's description of his book as a "useful possession" to which he implicitly contrasts the magnificence of the "sempiternal monuments" of Periclean Athens. See Leo Strauss, *The City and Man* (Chicago: Rand McNally, 1964), p. 228. On the virtue of magnificence, see Aristotle, *Nicomachean Ethics* 1122b11-35.

This Lorenzo the Magnificent (1492-1519) was the son of Piero de' Medici (1471-1503) and the nephew of Giovanni, Pope Leo X (1475-1521). Piero and Pope Leo X were the sons of the famed Lorenzo the Magnificent (1449-1492). The younger, and lesser, Lorenzo attained to his state in Florence as a result of the elevation of his other uncle, Giuliano (1478-1516), to a French ducal title, Nemours. Lorenzo was subsequently named the Duke of Urbino (1516) by Leo X. In sum, he was a perfect example of someone who becomes a prince not by virtue but by fortune. That is, Lorenzo was in a situation similar to that of Cesare Borgia.

5. *suppellettile* — Also the furnishings of a house, office, etc., but it has the technical meaning of military equipment.

6. Machiavelli's most precious possession is his knowledge of human things. He says nothing concerning the knowledge of unchanging things.

7. That is, the many who approach princes. But Machiavelli is also referring to those who write on princes, as he makes clear in the next sentence when he speaks of those who discuss and regulate the government of princes. A long tradition existed of writing "Mirrors of Princes," extending back to Xenophon's *Cyropaedia,* outlining the education of a prince, and it is to this tradition that Machiavelli alludes. See *Discourses,* III.39.

8. *Animo* — Animo is translated by me chiefly as "mind." It is translated here, in Ch. IX, para. 4 and Ch. XXVI, the last para., as "spirit," and as "heart" in Ch. XXIII, para. 4. *Anima,* "soul," is never used in *The Prince* and *spirito* is used only once (Ch. XXVI). See Strauss, *Thoughts on Machiavelli,* p. 333 (n. 59 of Ch. IV). I translate *animoso* principally as "spirited."

9. *Lei* — The third person pronoun is used for formal address. I have chosen to emphasize the formality of Machiavelli's address to the Duke. See Ch. III, n.3, below.

10. Machiavelli has to bear "a great and continuous malignity of fortune." Thus, also, Cesare Borgia is deprived of success by "the extraordinary and extreme malignity of fortune" (see Ch. VII, below). A natural prince, on the other hand, can be deprived of his state only by "an extraordinary and excessive force" (Ch. II). See also *Discourses,* II. Pref., end.

4

OF PRINCIPATES[1]

I

HOW MANY KINDS OF PRINCIPATES THERE ARE AND BY WHAT MODES[2] THEY ARE ACQUIRED*

All the states,[3] all the dominions that have had and have imperium[4] over men, have been and are either republics or principates. Principates are either hereditary, in which the blood[5] of their lords has for a long time been princely, or else they are new. The new are either all new, as was Milan for Francesco Sforza,[6] or are like members adjoined to the hereditary state of the prince who acquires[7] them, as is the Kingdom of Naples for the King of Spain.[8] Dominions thus acquired are either habituated to living under a prince or are used to being free; and they are acquired either with the arms of others or with one's own, either by fortune or by virtue.[9]

Quot Sint Genera Principatuum et Quibus Modis Acquirantur

Notes

1. *De Principatibus* — I use the term "principate" throughout because it calls to mind (in accordance with Machiavelli's intention) the Roman principate. What Machiavelli is concerned with is not a regime and certainly not a territory, but the virtue of the "first man," whose virtue is such that he is able to make a state for himself almost anywhere or anytime that he is.

2. *modo* — translated throughout as "mode." Machiavelli, like a good weaver (see Ch. II), weaves a texture in which certain recurrent patterns serve as important accents in the completed design. I wish to preserve these patterns as much as is possible.
   One of Machiavelli's most significant phrases is, of course, *"modi et ordini nuovi"* (new modes and orders). See the Introduction, Ch. VI below, and *Discourses* I. Preface. Leo Strauss, in his review of Fr. Leslie J. Walker's translation of Machiavelli's *Discourses* (New Haven: Yale University Press, 1950) 2 vols., points out that: *"Modus ed ordo* is the Latin translation of Aristotle's *taxis* (cf. Thomas in *Politics* 1289a 2-6, liber IV. lectio I). Machiavelli then sets out to discover, not a new method of studying political things, but new political 'arrangements' in regard to both structures and polities . . ." ("Walker's Machiavelli," *Review of Metaphysics,* VI:3 [1953], 440).

3. *lo stato* — "the state," as this word will be translated throughout, even where it would seem incorrect current usage. Machiavelli is here using a term the meaning of which today arises, in great part, out of the way Machiavelli uses it. It is important, therefore, to see clearly what he means by it, and this one can do only by preserving his original usage. See the Introduction for a discussion of his use of this term.

4. *l'imperio* — translated here, in most cases, as imperium, in its original meaning as command in war and the interpretation and execution of the law within the jurisdiction of that command. Execution of the law especially means, of course, execution of the

death penalty. See the *Oxford Classical Dictionary,* 2nd ed., for a discussion of the term. In a few places the context indicates that the empire, in the sense of dominion over territory, is meant.

5. *il sangue* — What the new prince must do with "the blood" is an important theme. I have, therefore, translated *il sangue* as "blood" throughout. Among other things, the blood has to do with the hold of tradition upon human beings.

6. Francesco Sforza (1401-1466) overthrew the Ambrosian Republic of Milan in 1450. See. Ch. XII, nn. 9, 10 and 12, below.

7. *acquista (acquistare)* — translated throughout as "acquire." He uses this word four times, in this very short chapter, three times in the body and its Latin equivalent in the title. He also uses it in the first sentence of the Epistle Dedicatory. See Ch. III below, where the "desire to acquire" is spoken of as "very natural and ordinary." It is perhaps *the* natural and ordinary passion of all human beings.

8. Ferdinand the Catholic of Spain agreed to divide the Kingdom of Naples with Louis XII of France by the Treaty of Granada in 1500. But in 1504 he drove the French out of Naples and joined it to Spain as a vice-royalty. See Ch. XXI, n. 2, below.

9. *la virtù* — translated throughout as "virtue." A deliberate ambiguity as what is meant by "virtue" is thereby preserved. See the Introduction for a discussion of this term. See also Ch. VI, n. 2, and Ch. XXI, n. 1, below.

II

OF HEREDITARY PRINCIPATES*

I shall omit the discussion[1] of republics, because on another occasion I discussed them at length.[2] I shall turn only to the principate, and go on weaving according to the order written above,[3] disputing how one is able to govern and to maintain these principates.

I say, then, that in maintaining hereditary states accustomed to the blood of their prince, the difficulties are very minor compared to those which are to be found in the new [state]; because it suffices [the hereditary prince] not to omit the order of his ancestors,[4] and, moreover, with respect to accidents, to wait for the opportune moment to act.[5] In this mode, if such a prince is of ordinary industry, he always maintains himself in his state, unless there is an extraordinary and excessive force which deprives him of it; and, deprived of it though he might be, let the usurper have some mishap and he reacquires it.

We have in Italy, for example, the Duke of Ferrara, who stood up to the assaults of the Venetians in '84, and those of Pope Julius in '10, for no causes[6] other than that he was ancient in that dominion.[7] For the natural prince[8] has fewer causes and less

*De Principatibus Hereditariis

necessity to offend; from whence it follows that he must be more loved; and if extraordinary vices do not make him hated, it is reasonable that they[9] would naturally have goodwill toward him. And in the antiquity and continuity of the dominion the memories and causes for innovations are extinguished; because one change always leaves the toothing for the building of another.[10]

Notes

1. *ragionare* — The work is, among other things, a reasoning or disputation, that is, the formal presentation of a thesis. He thus uses the term *ragionare* or reasoning in the first sentence of this chapter, emphasizing the scholastic character of the work. See Ch. XII, the first paragraph, below.

2. Machiavelli is, of course, referring to the *Discourses on the First Ten Books of Titus Livy,* the most useful translation of which is that of Fr. Leslie J. Walker, S. J. (New Haven: Yale University Press, 1950), 2 vols. See Ch. I, n. 2, above.

3. According to the topics given in Ch. I, of which there are 13. On weaving and the art of statesmanship, see Plato, *Statesman* 279-286A.

4. That is, the "form" of the city, the regime or *politeia* as founded by his ancestors. See Aristotle, *Politics* 1276b3-11.

5. *temporeggiare con gli accidenti* — "to wait for the opportune moment to act." The meaning can be either "to temporize," that is, to comply with the circumstances of the time or to yield temporarily and procrastinate; or it can mean, *"aspettare il momento opportuno per agire,"* — as I have translated it, "to wait for the opportune moment to act." Cf. *Discourses,* I.37, where it is used in the first sense. The hereditary prince would seem to have to do more than temporize; he must also know when to act if he is to keep his state.

6. *cagione* — Translated throughout as "cause," except in Ch.

XIV (p. 88). Machiavelli seems to distinguish a "cause" *(cagione)* from a "reason" *(ragione);* for causes are what move men to act, whereas reasons are what men say about what moves them. Reasons, in brief, are what men are able to say about causes. See Harvey C. Mansfield, Jr., *Machiavelli's New Modes and Orders,* pp. 259-273.

7. Machiavelli speaks of two Dukes of Ferrara as if they were one: Ercole d'Este (1431-1505) and his son Alfonso d'Este (1476-1534). It should be noted Machiavelli is somewhat inaccurate about historical facts throughout *The Prince.* The events to which he alludes are as follows: Venice and the Pope (Sixtus IV) declared war on Ercole d'Este in 1482, but failed to dislodge him and peace was concluded in 1484. In 1510, Pope Julius II decided to abandon the alliance with France (the League of Cambrai), which had been directed against Venice, and concluded a separate peace with the Venetians. Alfonso failed to follow him. The French were driven from Italy (see Ch. XI below), and Alfonso was sent into exile by Julius — that is, Alfonso did not quite "stand up" to Julius. Alfonso was subsequently restored to his duchy by Pope Leo X.

8. A natural prince is one to whose blood or lineage the people have become accustomed. But Machiavelli seems to suggest that the natural prince may also be something other: he is one who is born by fortune a prince, and then is able to take advantage of whatever accidents befall him.

9. they — since Machiavelli is addressing a prince, he speaks of the many (that is, the people), simply as "they."

10. *addentellato* — The toothing is a technical architectural term denoting bricks or stones left alternately projecting at the end of walls of buildings so that additions may easily be made.

III

OF MIXED PRINCIPATES*

But the new principate is that which presents difficulties. And
first, if it is not all new but is like a member[1] (so that one can call
the whole which has been brought together, as it were, mixed), its
alterations arise in the beginning from a natural difficulty, which
is [to be found] in all new principates; and that is that men
willingly change masters believing [they will] better [them-
selves], and this belief makes them take up arms against
them; whereby they deceive themselves for they then experience
that they have the worse. That follows from another natural and
ordinary necessity, and that is that he needs must always hurt
those whose new prince he becomes, and hurt them with men-at-
arms[2] and with infinite other injuries that the new acquisition
drags along with it. In this mode you[3] have as enemies all those
whom you have hurt in seizing that principate; and you are not
able to maintain as friends those who have placed you there, being
unable to satisfy them in the mode that they had expected and by
your not being able to use strong medicines against them, being
obligated to them, for even if one has the most powerful of armies, one always has need of the favor of the inhabitants of a

*De Principatibus Mixtis

province to enter it. For these causes, Louis XII, King of France, quickly seized and quickly lost Milan, and Ludovico's own forces, the first time that France lost Milan, were enough to take it from him;[4] because those people who had opened the gates to him, finding themselves deceived in their opinion of that future good which they had expected, could not put up with the annoyances of [having] a new prince.[5]

It is very true that when countries that have rebelled are acquired for the second time, they are then lost with more difficulty; for the ruler, taking the occasion of their rebellion, has less concern for them and secures himself by punishing delinquents, exposing suspects, and providing for himself where he is weakest. In this mode, to have [the King of] France[6] lose Milan the first time, it was enough for a Duke Ludovico to make a noise on her confines; but to have him lose it a second time, it was needful that all the world come against him, and that his armies be extinguished or driven out of Italy; this arises from the causes mentioned above. Nevertheless, the first and the second time, it was taken from him.

The general causes for the first [loss] have already been discussed; it remains now to state those of the second, and to see what remedies there were for [the King], and what there are for someone who might be in the same situation as [he], so that he may better maintain himself in his acquisition than did France.

I say therefore that those states which are acquired, if annexed to the state anciently held of him who acquired them, are either of the same province[7] and the same language, or they are not. When they are, it is very easy to hold them, and especially so when they are not used to living free; and to possess them securely, it is enough to have extinguished the line of the prince who ruled over them, because, among other things, if former conditions are maintained and there are no differences in customs, men live quietly, as one sees Burgundy, Brittany, Gascony, and Normandy have done, which have for so long been with France; and although there are some differences in language, nevertheless their customs are similar, and they have been able easily to comport one with another. And he who acquires them, wishing to keep them, ought to have two concerns: the one that the blood of their ancient prince be extinguished; the other, that neither their laws nor their taxes be altered; so that in a very short time it becomes all one body with the ancient principate.

But when one acquires states in a province [which is] different [from one's own] in language, customs and orders, here are [to be found] difficulties, and here is there need of great fortune and great industry to hold them. And one of the greatest, quickest and most effective of remedies would be that the person who has acquired them go there to live. This would make that possession more secure and more enduring: as the Turk has done in Greece — and if he had not gone there to live, it would not have been possible to hold it, despite all the other orders observed by him to maintain that state. For being there, they themselves see the disorders as they arise, and they are then able quickly to remedy them; but not being there they hear of them only when they become great and when there is no more remedy. Moreover, the province is not despoiled by your[8] officials; the subjects are satisfied by the near recourse to the prince, whereupon they have more cause to love him, wishing to be good, and wishing to be otherwise, to fear him. And if any of the powers external [to that province] would want to assault his state, they would have to have greater respect; so that living there, he can lose it only with the greatest difficulty.

The other best remedy[9] is to send colonies to one or two places which are, as it were, the shackles of that state;[10] for it is necessary either to do this or to have men-at-arms and infantry there. On colonies, not much is spent; and without any or with little spending, he can send and keep them, and he hurts only those whose fields and houses are taken and given to the new inhabitants, and the former are but a small part of that state; and those whom he

13

hurts, remaining dispersed and poor, can never injure him. All the others have, on the one hand, no hurt given to them, and because of this they should remain quiet, and on the other hand, they will be afraid of making a mistake, for fear that what had happened to those who had been despoiled might also happen to them. I conclude that such colonies do not cost anything, are more faithful, hurt less; and those who are hurt cannot do injury, being poor and dispersed, as has been said. For this to be noted: that one has either to caress men or to extinguish them, for if they can take revenge for light offenses, they cannot do so for grave ones; if one has to do hurt to men it should be in such a mode that there is no fear of vengeance. But in having men-at-arms there, instead of colonies, one spends much more, having to consume in garrisons all the income of that state; in such a mode that the acquisition turns into a loss; and he hurts many more, by having [continually] to change the quarters of his army,[11] which thereby injures all of the state. Everyone feels the hardship, and everyone becomes his enemy; and they are enemies who can do him injury, because although beaten, they remain in their own home. Hence, in every way, this [remedy] of a garrison is as useless as that of colonies is useful.

He who is in a different province [from his own], as has been said, ought also to become the leader and the defender of the neighboring lesser powers, to contrive to weaken the powerful of that [different province], and to prevent that, by some accident, there should enter a foreigner more powerful than he. Now it will always come about that he[12] will be brought in by those who, either from too much ambition or from fear, are malcontents, as happened formerly when the Aetolians brought the Romans into Greece — and in every other province that the latter entered, they were brought in by the provincials. And the order of these things is such that as soon as a powerful foreigner enters a province, all the less powerful therein adhere to him, moved by the envy they have against him who had held power over them: such that, with respect to these weaker powers, he does not have to endure any toil to gain them because they immediately and willingly make themselves wholly one with the state that he has acquired there. He has only to think about how they should not have too much force and too much authority; and he can, with his forces and their favor, easily put down those who are powerful, so that he remains, in all things, the arbiter of that province. And he who does not manage well this part, will quickly lose that which he has acquired; and while he holds it, he will have infinite difficulties and vexations in it.

The Romans, in the provinces they took, observed well these matters:[13] they sent colonies, kept and provided for the less powerful without increasing their power, put down the powers, and never let powerful foreigners gain a reputation. And I wish the province of Greece to suffice as the only example of this point: the Achaeans and the Aetolians were kept and provided for by them; the Kingdom of Macedonia was put down; Antiochus was driven out; nor did the merits of the Achaeans nor those of the Aetolians ever make them permit any of these to increase their state: nor did Philip's persuasions ever induce them to be friendly to him without [first] putting him down; nor could the power of Antiochus make them consent that he should hold any state in that province. For the Romans, in these cases, did all that wise princes ought to do; which is, to have regard not only for present disorders,[14] but also for future ones, and with all industry to anticipate and provide for them; because, when one foresees them from afar, one can easily remedy them; but if you wait until they are near the medicine is not in time, for the malady has become incurable.

And it comes of this, as the physicians say of the fever,[15] that, in the beginning of one's illness it is easy to cure but difficult to know; but, the medication not having been known in the beginning, with the progress of time, the fever becomes easy to know but difficult to cure. Thus it happens also in the things of state; for when one knows from afar (which is given only to a prudent[16] one) the ills that are being born, they are cured quickly; but when, by their not having been known, they are left to grow in such a mode that everyone knows them, then there is no more remedy.

But the Romans, seeing from afar the inconveniences, always remedied them; and they never let them follow in order to avoid a war, because they knew that war is not to be avoided, but is only deferred to the advantage of others; therefore they wished rather to make war with Philip and Antiochus in Greece, so that it should not have to be waged with them in Italy; and though they were able at the moment to avoid both the one and the other, they did not want to do so. Nor did that which is ordinarily in the mouth of the wise of our times, "to enjoy the benefit of time," ever please them, but [they chose] rather [to take] such benefit [as came] from their virtue and prudence; for time drives forward everything, and can bring along with it the good as well as the bad, and the bad as well as the good.

But let us turn to France, and examine if he did any one of the things said; and I shall speak of Louis and not of Charles,[17] because, as he had longer possession of Italy, his progresses[18] are much better seen; and you[19] will see how he has done the contrary of those things which ought to be done in order to have a state in a different province.

King Louis was brought into Italy by the ambition of the Venetians, who wanted to gain half the state of Lombardy by his coming. I do not want to blame the part taken by the King; for wanting to begin gaining a foothold in Italy, and having no allies in that province — on the contrary, having all the doors closed against him because of the behavior of King Charles — he was forced to make what alliances he could; and this well-made choice would have succeeded if he had not made an error in the management of other [affairs]. The King, then, acquired Lombardy; immediately he regained that reputation which King Charles had lost. Genoa surrendered, the Florentines became allies; the Marquis of Mantua, the Duke of Ferrara, the Bentivogli, the Lady of Forlì, the Lords of Faenza, Pesaro, Rimini, Camerino, Piombino, the Lucchesians, Pisanese, Sienese, everyone came to meet him in order to be his friend.[20] And now the Venetians were able to consider the temerity of their part, which was: in order to acquire some towns in Lombardy, they made the King the lord of a third of Italy.[21]

Let one consider now with what little difficulty the King could have kept his reputation in Italy, if he had observed the rules written above, and secured and defended all who were his friends, who were of a very great number, but because they were weak and therefore fearful, some fearful of the Church and others of the Venetians, they were necessitated always to support him; and by means of them he could easily have secured himself against those who remained great. But no sooner was he in Milan than he did the contrary by giving aid to Pope Alexander[22] so that the latter might seize the Romagna. Nor did he [the King] perceive that with this deliberation he weakened himself, removing his own friends and those who had been thrown into his lap from himself, and made the Church great, adding to the spiritual, which already gives to her so much authority, so much of the temporal.[23] And the first error having been made, he was constrained to continue, so that, to put an end to the ambition of Alexander and to prevent his becoming lord of Tuscany, he was constrained to come to Italy. It was not sufficient for him that he made the Church great and removed friends from himself, but by wanting the Kingdom of Naples, he divided it with the King of Spain; and where, before, he was the arbiter of Italy, he let enter a partner, so that the ambitious of that province and those ill-affected toward him would have recourse to another; and instead of continuing to allow the King of Naples to be his tributary, he removes him, in order to put someone there who could chase him out.

It is a thing truly very natural and ordinary to desire to acquire; and when men who are able to do so do it, they are always praised or not blamed; but when they are not able and yet want to do so in every mode, here is the error and the blame. If France, then, was able with his forces to attack Naples, he ought to have done so; if he was not able to do so, he ought not to have divided it. And if he had divided Lombardy with the Venetians, that merited excuse, for he put his foot into Italy by having done so; the other division merits blame, by its not being excused by this necessity.

Louis committed, then, these five errors: he extinguished the weaker powers; he increased the power of someone already powerful in Italy; he brought in an extremely powerful foreigner; he did not go to live there; he did not plant colonies.

And yet these errors might not have hurt him while he was still living, if he had not committed the sixth: that of taking the state away from the Venetians. For if he had not made the Church great, nor put Spain into Italy, it would have been very reasonable and necessary to bring [the Venetians] down; but having made these [other] choices first, he ought never to have consented to their ruin, for being powerful, they would always have kept others off from venturing into Lombardy, because the Venetians would not have given their consent to any one else entering Lombardy except themselves, nor would the others have wanted to take it from France in order to give it to the Venetians: and they would not have had the courage to go against these two [France and Venice] together. And if someone should say, King Louis ceded the Romagna to Alexander and the Kingdom [of Naples] to Spain to avoid a war, I respond, for the reasons[24] mentioned above, one ought never to permit a disorder to follow to avoid a war, for one does not avoid it and it is only deferred to your[25] disadvantage. And if some others would allege the faith [pledged],[26] whereby the King had become obligated to the Pope to undertake for him that enterprise [of the Romagna] for the resolution of his marriage and the hat of Rouen, I respond with what shall be said below by me about the faith of princes and how one ought to observe it.[27]

King Louis, then, lost Lombardy, because he did not observe any of the rules observed by others who have taken provinces and have wanted to keep them. Nor is any of this a miracle, but is very ordinary and reasonable. And on this matter I spoke with Rouen at Nantes, when Valentino (that was how Cesare Borgia, son of Pope Alexander, was popularly called) seized the Romagna; for the Cardinal of Rouen saying to me that the Italians did not understand the things of war, I answered him that the French did not understand the things of the state, because if they did understand them, they would not have let the Church come into such greatness.[28] And experience has shown that the greatness of the Church and that of Spain in Italy has been caused by France, and his ruin caused by them. From this there may be drawn a general rule which never or rarely fails:[29] that he who is the cause of another's becoming powerful ruins himself; for that power is caused either by industry or by force, and the one and the other are suspect to him who has become powerful.

Notes

1. *membro* — In the archaic sense of a bodily part or organ. A member is not only a separable portion of a whole, it is also an independent constituent part of the whole.

2. *gente d'arme* — Men-at-arms are heavily armored mounted soldiers. They are to be distinguished from regular cavalry and infantry. The mercenaries were men-at-arms for causes Machiavelli outlines in Ch. XII, below.

3. *tu* — This is the first time Machiavelli addresses the prince familiarly and as an equal. We have moved far from the low place Machiavelli occupied in the Epistle Dedicatory. On Machiavelli's use of the courteous second person, see n. 19 of this chapter.

4. Ludovico Sforza, il Moro (1450-1510), was Duke of Milan from 1494 to 1500.

5. *non potevano sopportare e fastidii del nuovo principe* — The emphasis is placed on the inevitable petty difficulties which arise from simply being a new prince. The beginning of the violent changes which threw not only Italy but all of Europe into disorder was the invasion of Italy by Charles VIII, King of France, in 1494 (see Ch. XXV, below). Charles (1470-1498) undertook his Italian expedition to lay claim to Naples in virtue of the rights to that Kingdom transmitted by the House of Anjou to the French royal family. His invasion was, however, short-lived and was significant only because his successor, Louis XII (1462-1515), continued the policy of asserting French interest in Italian affairs. The chronology of contemporary events that Machiavelli comments upon in *The Prince* begins with the invasion of Charles VIII and continues with the taking of Milan by Louis in September, 1499. Ludovico re-entered Milan in February, 1500, and was betrayed by his Swiss mercenaries. The French recaptured Milan in April — Georges d'Amboise, the Cardinal of Rouen, was sent by Louis XII to be governor over that city. In 1500 a treaty with Spain partitioning Naples (Treaty of Granada) was concluded. The war of France with Naples and the capture of that city occurred in August, 1501; the war between the French and the Spanish over Naples occurred from 1502-1505, with Ferdinand of Aragon becoming King of Naples by the Treaty of Blois, October, 1505. In Chapter VII, Machiavelli takes up the events which arise from Cesare Borgia's actions in 1501-1503.

Machiavelli's *Florentine Histories* (1525) go back to the beginnings of Florence and end with the death of Lorenzo the Magnificent in 1492; that is, they end immediately before the entrance of Charles VIII into Italy.

Francesco Guicciardini begins his *History of Italy* with a description of conditions in 1494:

> The calamities of Italy began (and I say this so that I may make known what her condition was before, and the causes from which so many evils arose), to the greater sorrow and terror of all men, at a

time when circumstance seemed universally most propitious and fortunate. It is indisputable that since the Roman Empire, weakened
largely by the decay of her ancient customs, began to decline more
than a thousand years ago from that greatness to which it had risen
with marvellous virtue and good fortune, Italy had never known such
prosperity or such a desirable condition as that which it enjoyed in all
tranquillity in the year of Our Lord 1490 and the years immediately
before and after. For, all at peace and quietness, cultivated no less in
the mountainous and sterile places than in the fertile regions and
plains, knowing no other rule than that of its own people, Italy was
not only rich in population, merchandise and wealth, but she was
adorned to the highest degree by the magnificence of many princes,
by the splendour of innumerable noble and beautiful cities, by the
throne and majesty of religion; full of men most able in the administration of public affairs, and of noble minds learned in every
branch of study and versed in every worthy art and skill. Nor did she
lack military glory according to the standards of those times; and being so richly endowed, she deservedly enjoyed among all other
nations a most brilliant reputation. (*History of Italy and History of
Florence,* trans. by Cecil Grayson and ed. and abridged by John R.
Hale [New York: Twayne Publishers, 1964], pp. 85-6.)

On Louis XII, see *Discourses,* I.38; II.15, 22, 24; III. 15, 31, 44. On
the nature of France, see *Discourses,* I.16, 55, 58; II.6, 8, 19; III.1,
36, 41, 43. See also Chs. XIX and XXV, below. On France in Italy,
see *Discourses,* I.12, 29, 59; II.16, 17, 18, 24; III.10, 11, 15, 31, 44.
See also the *"Ritratto delle cose di Francia,"* and *"De Natura
Gallorum,"* in *Tutte le Opere di Niccolò Machiavelli,* edited by
Francesco Flora and Carlo Cordié (Verona: Arnoldo Mondadori,
1968), pp. 667-702.

6. France — Machiavelli speaks of the King of France as France.
He is, of course, primarily concerned with the prince, although it
must be noted that France is also a province as is indicated in the
subsequent paragraph and especially in Ch. IV, below.

7. A province appears to be a natural division of the human race,
referring to a people similar in descent, language and customs. A
people is formed by the place in which they live, as the Turks and

the French are differently constituted by the differences between Asia and Europe (see Ch. IV, below). That is, the province is the natural substratum upon which the state, the artificial being, is constructed.

8. See Ch. VI, n. 1, below.

9. There are two "best" remedies: to go there and live, or to send colonies. Machiavelli does perhaps consider colonies to be more practicable, but of all the remedies these are the two best. Which one is to be adopted clearly depends upon the circumstances of the prince.

10. That is, the key points which, being held, would keep the people in subjection.

11. Quarters have to be changed, of course, because of the burden upon the people.

12. That is, the powerful foreigner.

13. For the policy of the Romans in Greece, see Montesquieu, *Considerations of the Causes of the Greatness of the Romans and Their Decline,* translated by David Lowenthal, Cornell paperbacks (Ithaca, N.Y.: Cornell University Press, 1968), Chs. V and VI. See *Discourses* II.1,4.

14. *scandoli* — This term may be translated "scandals" in the now obsolete meaning of an untoward turn of troublesome circumstances that leads to public clamor.

15. That is, consumptive or tubercular fever.

16. *prudente* — *Prudente* and *prudenzia* are translated throughout as "prudent" and "prudence." In keeping with what was said in the Epistle Dedicatory, Machiavelli's concern with knowledge of the human things leads him to emphasize prudence, that intellectual virtue which is concerned with knowledge of the changeable things. See Aristotle, *Nicomachean Ethics* 1140a24-1140b30, 1141b1-1142a30. See also Ch. VI, n. 2, below.

17. Of Louis XII of France and not of Charles VIII, for which see n. 5 above, this chapter.

18. Progresses, as in royal journeys or tours which are marked by pomp and pageant.

19. *vedrete* — Machiavelli uses the courteous form of the second person. Strauss suggests that this is because he is no longer addressing the prince but the reader "whose interest is primarily theoretical" (*Thoughts on Machiavelli,* p. 77). Note will be made of whether the familiar or courteous "you" is being used.

20. These were respectively: Francesco Gonzaga, Marquis of Mantua; Ercole I d'Este, Duke of Ferrara; Giovanni Bentivoglio, Lord of Bologna; Caterina Riario Sforza, Lady of Forlì; Astorre Manfredi, Lord of Faenza; Giovanni Sforza, Lord of Pesaro; Pandolfo Malatesta, Lord of Rimini; Giulio Cesare da Varano, Lord of Camerino; Jacopo IV d'Appiano, Lord of Piombino. All of these little *signori* were despoiled of their possessions or killed by Cesare Borgia between 1500 and 1502. See Ch. VII, below.

21. Venice was promised possession of the Ghiara d'Adda, that is, the towns and territories of Brescia, Bergamo, Crema, and Cremona.

22. Alexander VI, born Rodrigo Borgia (1431-1503), was pope from 1492 to 1503. His actions, and those of his son, Cesare Borgia, interest Machiavelli for they almost succeeded in transforming the Church into a political power. On Alexander and Cesare, see Ch. XXVI, n. 2, below. Alexander VI began "to draw the sword" with the seizure of the Romagna. As is indicated, he could only have done this with the help of the French king.

23. One should note that he never uses the word power, which is otherwise very much in evidence in this chapter, whenever he mentions the Church. Not until the end of Chapter XI does he explicitly say that the Church has power. The Church has greatness (*grandezza*) but not power, until the papacy of Leo X when the

pontificate is said to be powerful; that is, not until the papacy of Leo X does the Church have arms. See the Introduction, above.

24. *ragioni* — Translated throughout as reasons. Here, what was previously referred to as "causes" become "reasons." For the distinction between "cause" and "reason" see Ch. II, n. 6, above.

25. The second person familiar is used.

26. *fede* — Translated throughout as "faith." Here it refers to the promise made by Louis XII in return for the Pope's annulment of his marriage to Jeanne Valois, the daughter of King Louis XI, and the raising of the Bishop of Rouen, Georges d'Amboise, to the cardinalate.

27. See Ch. XVIII, below, on the faith of princes.

28. This conversation evidently occurred during the first diplomatic mission of Machiavelli to France from July to November, 1500.

29. A "general rule which never or rarely fails" is to be distinguished from a "mode which never fails" (see Ch. XXII, below). It would seem that a general rule which tells us a truth about human things is applied through the adoption of a certain mode of action. For example, a general rule is that cruelty must be used. But how that cruelty is used depends upon the modes a prince adopts. In turn, these modes depend upon the prince's "humor," that is, whether he is inclined to be harsh or gentle, impetuous or cautious. See Ch. XXV, below, and the Introduction.

IV

WHY THE KINGDOM OF DARIUS
WHICH ALEXANDER HAD SEIZED
DID NOT REBEL AGAINST HIS SUCCESSORS
AFTER THE DEATH OF ALEXANDER*

Having considered the difficulties which are encountered in holding on to a state newly acquired, one might marvel how it came to pass that Alexander the Great[1] became lord of Asia in a few years and, not having yet fully conquered it, died; whereupon it would seem reasonable that the whole state should have rebelled. Nevertheless, the successors of Alexander maintained it; and they did not, in holding it, have any difficulties other than those which arose among themselves from their own ambitions. I respond[2] that the principates of which we have memory are found to be governed in two diverse modes: either by a prince, and all the others are his servants who, being ministers by his grace and permission, help him to govern that kingdom; or by a prince and barons, the latter having their rank not by the grace of the lord, but by the antiquity of their blood. These barons have their own states and subjects who not only acknowledge them as their lords, but have them in their natural affections. States which are governed by a prince and servants hold their prince in more authority, because in all of his province there is no one recognized as his

*Cur Darii Regnum Quod Alexander Occupaverat a Successoribus Suis Post Alexandri Mortem non Defecit

superior; and if they do obey any others, they obey them as ministers and officials, and bear them no particular love.

In our time, the examples of these two different kinds of government are those of the Turk and of the King of France.[3] The whole monarchy of the Turk is governed by one lord — the others are his servants. And dividing his kingdom into Sangiachi,[4] he sends to these [districts] different administrators, changing and placing them as seems fit to him. But the King of France is placed in the midst of a multitude of lords who of old are recognized in that state by their [respective] subjects and are loved by them. They have their privileges and these the king cannot take away without danger to himself. Whoever considers, then, the one and the other of these states, will find that it is difficult to acquire the state of the Turk, but [once] conquered, it is easy to hold. And, you[5] will find, on the contrary, that it is in some respects easier to take the state of France, but that it is with great difficulty that one holds on to it.

The causes of the difficulty in being able to occupy the kingdom of the Turk are that one cannot be called in by the princes of that kingdom, nor can one hope to facilitate one's enterprise through the rebellion of those around him. This arises from the reasons mentioned above; for, all being slaves and obliged to him, they are corrupted with more difficulty; and if one could indeed corrupt them, one cannot hope that they would be of much use, as they are unable to draw the people after them for the reasons given. Hence it is necessary for whoever attacks the Turk to think that he will find him wholly united, and that he needs must hope more from his own forces than from the others' disorders. But, if [the Turk] were conquered and broken in the field, in such a mode that he is not able to re-form his armies, then one does not have to doubt anything other than the blood of the prince, which, when extinguished, leaves no one to fear, since no others have credit with the people. And as the conqueror before the victory could not put his hopes in them,[6] so he ought not, afterwards, fear them.

The contrary happens in kingdoms governed like France, for you[7] can enter them easily, gaining to yourself some barons of the kingdom. For one always finds some malcontents and those who desire to innovate; these, for the reasons said, are able to open to you the way to that state and facilitate your victory. Whereupon, your desire to maintain it draws after it infinite difficulties, alike with those who have aided you and with those whom you have oppressed. Nor is it enough for you to extinguish the blood of the prince, for there remain those lords who make themselves heads of new disturbances; and being unable to make them content or to extinguish them, you lose that state whenever the occasion comes.

Now, if you[8] will consider the nature of Darius's government,[9] you will find it similar to the kingdom of the Turk. Therefore it was necessary for Alexander first to smash it all and seize the field; after which victory, with Darius dead, the state was left secure for Alexander for the reasons discussed above. And if his successors had remained united they could have enjoyed it indolently; nor did there arise in that kingdom any tumults other than those which they themselves provoked. But it is impossible to possess states ordered like that of France with such quiet. From whence arose each of the many rebellions of Spain, of France, and of Greece against the Romans, because of the many principates which existed in those states. While the memory of them endured, the Romans were always uncertain of these possessions; but with their memory extinguished, with the power and the long duration of the Empire, they became secure possessors. And they possessed them even when they were fighting among themselves afterwards, each drawing a following from a part of these provinces, according to the authority he had in them;[10] and, the blood of their lords having been extinguished, these provinces would not recognize anyone who was not a Roman. Having considered, then, all these things, no one should marvel at the ease Alexander had in holding on to the state of Asia, and the difficulties the others have had in conserving their acquisition, like

Pyrrhus and many others. This does not arise from the greater or lesser virtue of the conqueror, but from the difference in the subject [province].[11]

Notes

1. On Alexander III, the Great (356-323 B.C.) see the *Discourses,* I.1, 20, 26, 58; II.8, 10, 27, 31; III.6, 13.

2. *Respondo* — One is again reminded of the scholastic character of the treatise. See Ch. II, n. 1, above.

3. On how France got its name, see *Discourses,* II.8. On the Turk, see Ch. XIX, n. 10, below.

4. An administrative district, the original meaning of the word seems to be a "banner" or "flag."

5. *troverrete* — The courteous second person is used. See Ch. III, n. 19, above.

6. Them — that is, the people.

7. The second person familiar is used. See Ch. VI, n.1, below.

8. *considerrete, troverrete* — The courteous second person is used.

9. This is Darius III (380-330 B.C.), the last Achaemenid Emperor.

10. During the civil wars, 88-42 B.C., Machiavelli is referring to the leaders of the factions, Marius, Sulla, Pompey, Caesar, etc.

11. The different natures of the peoples are, as it were, the different kinds of matter which the prince must, with his virtue, mold into his own modes and orders. See Chs. VI, n.5; XVII, n. 15; and XXV, n. 3, below. See *Discourses,* III.43, I.11, and III.8.

V

IN WHAT MODE CITIES OR PRINCIPATES MUST BE ADMINISTERED WHICH BEFORE THEY WERE SEIZED USED TO LIVE BY THEIR OWN LAWS*

When the acquired states, as has been said, are accustomed to living under their own laws and in liberty, there are for those who want to hold them three modes [of proceeding]: the first, to ruin them; the other, to go to live there personally; the third, to let them live under their own laws, levying tribute, and creating there a state of a few who will keep it friendly to you.[1] Such a state, having been created by that prince, knows that it cannot stand without his friendship and power, and that it must do everything to maintain him; and one holds a city used to living in liberty more easily by means of its citizens than in any other mode — if one wishes to preserve it.[2]

As examples, there are the Spartans and the Romans.[3] The Spartans held Athens and Thebes by creating there a state of a few[4] — yet they lost them again. The Romans, in order to hold Capua, Carthage and Numantia,[5] destroyed them — and they did not lose them. They wanted to hold Greece somewhat as the Spartans had, freeing them and leaving them to their own laws, and they did not succeed. In such a mode they were constrained to destroy many cities in that province in order to hold it.[6]

*Quomodo Administrandae Sint Civitates vel Principatus, Qui Antequam Occuparentur, Suis Legibus Vivebant

29

For, in truth, there is not any sure mode of possessing [such cities], other than to ruin them. And whoever becomes the master of a city accustomed to living in liberty, and does not destroy it — he waits to be destroyed by it. For it always has as a refuge in rebellion the name of liberty and its ancient orders, which are never forgotten either through length of time or through benefits. And no matter what one does or provides for, if the inhabitants are not disunited or dispersed, they neither forget that name nor those orders, and immediately, upon every accident, they resort to them, as Pisa did one hundred years after being placed in servitude to the Florentines.[7]

But when cities or provinces are used to living under a prince, and that blood is extinguished, since they are on the one hand used to obedience and on the other are deprived of the old prince, they will not be able to agree upon choosing some one from among themselves [to rule], and they do not know how to live in liberty; in this mode they will be very late to take up arms, and a prince is able to win them over with more facility and assure himself of them. But in republics there is greater life, greater hate, more desire for vengeance; the memory of ancient liberty does not leave them, nor can it let them rest — so that the safest way is either to extinguish them or to live there.

Notes

1. The second person familiar is used.

2. The city is mentioned for the first time in this chapter, in connection with the question of liberty. It would seem that republics are especially cities, or that the modes and orders of liberty are found principally to exist in cities and not in such huge and amorphous political entities as empires. A city has a definite, limited form, and this is perhaps what is necessary for the existence of liberty. See Ch. IX, below, where a "civil order" is contrasted with an "absolute" one. The question raised at the end of

the first paragraph has to do with whether one wishes to preserve the constitution and laws of a city or not.

3. On the comparison between Sparta and Rome, see *Discourses*, I.2, 5-6.

4. Oligarchy, the régime of the few, was established in 404 B.C., with the conclusion of the Peloponnesian War.

5. Capua rebelled after Cannae (the greatest defeat inflicted on the Romans by Hannibal), and was destroyed in 211 B.C. by Rome. Carthage was destroyed in 146 B.C., in what is called the Third Punic War; and Numantia, in Spain, was destroyed in 133 B.C., ending Spain's resistance to Rome.

6. Corinth was completely destroyed by the Romans in 146 B.C.

7. Pisa was acquired by Florence in 1405. But in 1494 with the entrance of the French king, Charles VIII, the Pisans rebelled. Florence recaptured Pisa only in 1509, after a long war and infinite vexations.

VI

OF NEW PRINCIPATES WHICH BY ONE'S OWN ARMS AND VIRTUE ARE ACQUIRED*

No one should marvel if in my speaking of wholly new principates — those in which the prince and the state are alike new — I shall bring forward the greatest examples; since men always walk, as it were, in the ways beaten by others and proceed in their actions by imitations, being unable to keep wholly to the ways of others and unable to measure up to the virtue of those whom you[1] imitate, a prudent man ought always enter into the ways beaten by great men and imitate those who have been most excellent, so that, if your virtue does not reach up to there, at least it gives some odor of it; and to do as prudent archers[2] do, who, when the target they purpose to strike appears very far off and knowing nicely how much the virtue of their bow can do, they place their aim much higher than the intended target, not to reach such a height with their arrow, but so they may, by aid of so high an aim, attain their purpose.

I say, then, that in wholly new principates where there is a new prince, one finds them more or less difficult to keep according to whether the one who has acquired them is more or less virtuous. And because this event of a private man becoming a prince presupposes either virtue or fortune, it seems that the one or the

*De Principatibus Novis Qui Armis Propriis et Virtute Acquirantur

other of these things mitigates, in part, many difficulties; nevertheless, he who stands less on fortune better maintains himself. Things are also facilitated if the prince is constrained, by his lack of other states, to live there personally.

But in order to come to those who have become princes by their own virtue and not by fortune, I say that the most excellent are Moses, Cyrus, Romulus, Theseus, and the like.[3] And although one ought not to reason of Moses, he having been a mere executor of the things that were ordained by God, he ought yet to be admired, if only for the grace which made him worthy to speak with God. But let us consider Cyrus and the others who have acquired or founded kingdoms: you[4] will find them all wonderful; and if their particular actions and orders are considered, they seem not discrepant from those of Moses, who had so great a preceptor. And in examining their actions and life, one sees that fortune provided them with nothing other than the occasion which gave them the matter into which they could introduce whatever form they pleased; without that occasion the virtue of their mind would have been extinguished, and without that virtue the occasion would have come in vain.

It was necessary, then, for Moses to find the people of Israel in Egypt, enslaved and oppressed by the Egyptians, so that they, in order to escape their servitude, would be disposed to follow him. It was fitting that Romulus not remain in Alba, that he be exposed at birth, so that he might want to become king of Rome and founder of that fatherland. It was needful that Cyrus find the Persians malcontented with the imperium of the Medes, and the Medes soft and effeminate from long peace. Theseus would have been unable to demonstrate his virtue if he had not found the Athenians scattered [in the countryside]. These occasions, therefore, made these men happy, and their excellent virtue made the occasion known; whence their fatherland[5] was ennobled and became most happy.

These men, and those like them, who become princes by virtuous ways, acquire the principate with difficulty, but they hold it with facility; and the difficulties which they have in acquiring the principate arise, in part, from the new orders and modes that they are forced to introduce to found their state and security. And one ought to consider that nothing is more difficult to deal with nor more dubious of success nor more dangerous to manage than making oneself the head in the introduction of new orders: for the introducer's enemies are all those who have done well by the old orders, while his defenders are all those who would do well by the new orders, and they are lukewarm. That lukewarmness arises partly from fear of the adversaries who have the laws on their side, partly from the incredulity of men who do not in truth believe in the new things until they firmly experience them; whence it comes to pass that, whenever one's enemies have the occasion to attack, they do so with partisanship and the others' defense is lukewarm — in such a mode all who are associated with him are endangered.

And it is therefore necessary, if one wants to discuss this part well, to examine whether these innovators stand on their own or if they depend on others; that is to say, whether to conduct their work they need to beg, or are truly able to force. In the first case, they always come to evil and lead to nothing; but when they depend upon their own and are able to force, then there is rarely a time that they are endangered. Whence it comes to pass that all armed prophets conquer and the unarmed ones are ruined. For, in addition to the things said, the nature of the people is variable, and it is easy to persuade them of a thing, but difficult to keep them firm in that persuasion. Therefore, it is needful to order [affairs] in such a mode that when the people do not believe any more, one is able to make them believe by force.

Moses, Cyrus, Theseus and Romulus, had they been unarmed, would have been unable to make them long observe their constitutions, as in our times happened to Fra Girolamo Savonarola, who was ruined in his new orders when the multitude began not to believe them; and he had no way to hold firm those who had believed nor to make the unbelievers believe.[6] Therefore, such men as these have great difficulty in the conduct [of their enterprise], and all their perils are on the way, and they must with their virtue surmount them; but having surmounted them, and commencing to be held in veneration, having extinguished those who were envious of their qualities, they remain powerful, secure, honored, happy.

I want to add a lesser example to such high examples; but it is a good one if it will be taken in proper proportion to the former, and I want it to suffice for all similar cases — and this is Hiero of Syracuse.[7] That man, from a private [station], became prince of Syracuse; and again he did not have anything from fortune other than the occasion; for the Syracusans, being oppressed, elected him for their captain; whence he gained such merit that he was made their prince. And he had so much virtue, even in private fortune, that he who wrote of him said: "For that man lacked nothing for ruling but a kingdom."[8] That man extinguished the old militia, ordered the new; left ancient alliances, made new ones; and as soon as he had allies and soldiers of his own making, he was able to build any edifice on such a foundation: so that he endured much toil in acquiring and little in maintaining.

Notes

1. *tu imiti* — All the translations consulted but one translate this phrase as if it were in the third person, singular or plural. This shift from the third to the second person familiar also occurs most notably in Ch. III, para. 16; Ch. IV, para. 4; Ch. VII, para. 14; Ch. VIII, the last para.; Ch. IX, para. 4; Ch. XII, para. 2; Ch. XIII, paras. 1 and 3; Ch. XIV, paras. 1 and 3; Ch. XVII, para. 3; Ch. XIX, para. 12; Ch. XX, para. 2, and Ch. XXIV, the last para. The effect intended, I believe, is to remind us that this is a treatise which not only gives general counsel, but is addressed to a particular prince and therefore also gives particular counsel. See

Strauss, *Thoughts on Machiavelli,* pp. 62-63. On the use of the courteous second person, see Ch. III, n. 19, above.

2. *gli arcieri prudenti* — "the prudent archers." Machiavelli's understanding of the relationship of prudence to virtue is indicated by his use of the image of the archer and the bow. The "virtue" of the bow is the power or capacity of the bow to shoot an arrow, but it is the "prudence" of the archer which permits the best use of the bow. Virtue is here understood in instrumental terms; it is not a question of moral character but rather of the capacity to act. Prudence is also understood instrumentally; it is knowledge of how best to use whatever virtue one has, whatever the circumstance in which one finds oneself. Perhaps prudence is necessary to make virtue fully known. That prudence is the intellectual virtue whereby one perceives in the particular that which leads to the good, is a thought which does not seem to be present in Machiavelli. Prudence, to repeat, was understood by Aristotle as the perception of the good or end of human action in whatever particular circumstance one found oneself. Our modern notion of conscience is an approximation of the Aristotelian understanding, with the difference that the modern conscience seems not so much an intellectual activity as it is one of the sentiments. For Machiavelli, there seems to be no idea of the good which guides human action, and prudence therefore becomes not the knowing of the good in the particulars of human action, but rather intelligence in the service of whatever goods are desired by human beings. Prudence thus administers to one's ruling desires, and we have been told (in Ch. III), that "the natural and ordinary desire" is to acquire (see Ch. I, n. 7, above). See the Introduction for a discussion of *virtù.* Cf. Ch. XXI, n. 1, below.

3. The legendary and mythical character of these men's lives should be noted. The approximate dates of these men are: Moses, 1300 B.C.; Cyrus, 559-529 B.C.; Romulus, 735 B.C.; Theseus, 1200 B.C. Of these men, Cyrus seems to be the most "historical" in the

modern meaning of that word. Moses: *Discourses,* I.1, 9; II.8; III.30; Cyrus: *Discourses,* II.12, 13; III.20, 22, 39; Romulus: *Discourses,* I.1, 2, 9, 10, 11, 19, 49; Theseus: *Discourses,* I.1.

As to who would be included in the phrase "and the like" there is an indication in Ch. XIV that there are certain kinds of men who, like Xenophon, write about such men as Cyrus, Moses, Theseus, Romulus, etc. One wonders about the relative status of Xenophon to Cyrus. Who is being imitated, Cyrus or Xenophon's Cyrus?

4. *troverrete* —·The courteous second person is used. See Ch. III, n. 19, above.

5. *la patria* — the fatherland. The fatherland is, of course, a land —i.e. it is a term whose meaning seems to be connected with that of a province (see the Introduction and Ch. III, n. 7, above). As the patriotic song says, the citizen loves the "Land where my fathers died," its "rocks and rills," its "woods and templed hills." One notes an intermixing of the natural and the conventional in the words of the song, and that reflects exactly what we wish to convey about the meaning Machiavelli appears to attach to "the fatherland." We note that here in Chapter VI, where the term is first used and used twice, that the fatherland must be founded and it can be ennobled by the establishment of a certain kind of order. (The ennobling of one's fatherland is to found the orders which will make it powerful, and thus secured and honored — and if powerfu¦, secured, and honored, it cannot then but be happy.) A fatherland would seem to possess the characteristics of the state and the province alike. Patriotic love is not simply the love of the land into which one is born; one also loves a political order.

But Machiavelli indicates, especially in Chapter XXVI, that what he desires above all is liberty for *this* fatherland — for Italy but not for the orders which presently exist. We note that "fatherland" is a term which is especially used for cities, that is, for an order which provides for liberty or citizenship (see Ch. V, n. 2, above). As we see from Chapter XXVI, one's fatherland may be conquered, but let howsoever many centuries pass and one may still have an allegiance to an order which exists only in the memory (see Ch. V), and that order is one's fatherland. There is a hint that a province demands a certain kind of order, which order then becomes a fatherland — that is, that a certain fatherland is proper to a certain province (see Ch. IV, but note that Rome was able to extinguish the memory of previous orders in the provinces they took). A fatherland cannot therefore be identified with the state, for one may be born into a state for which one feels no love. A fatherland, or the order one loves, is the order wherein a human being finds himself at home. The founder of a state would wish above all then to make his state a fatherland. ("Fatherland" is used twice in Ch. VI, thrice in Ch. VIII, twice in Ch. IX, and once in Ch. XXVI. See also Ch. XXVI, n. 20, below.)

6. Savonarola (1452-1498) was a Dominican friar who captured the Florentine people with his prophetic sermons and who tried to establish Florence as a Christian republic. He actually ruled the Florentine republic with Piero Soderini (the Gonfaloniere) from 1494, but he became involved in a challenge to prove his prophetic gifts through an ordeal by fire. When the ordeal never came to pass because of bickering and delays, the people blamed Savonarola for the failure and turned against him. Opposed by the Franciscans, the Pope, and the followers of the Medici, he was hanged and burned in the Piazza della Signoria, May 23, 1498. See Ch. XII, n. 6, below.

7. Hiero II, tyrant of Syracuse (306-215 B.C.), reigned for 54 years. He was forced to conclude a peace with Rome (263) and remained from then on under Roman protection. See the *Discourses*, Dedication. See Ch. XIII, n. 13, below.

8. *Quid nihil illi deerat ad regnandum praeter regnum*. Two references have been given for this quotation: one is to Justin's compendium of Pompeius Trogus's *Historiae Philippicae*, a work which has otherwise been lost; the other is to Polybius's *Histories*, I.8 and VII.7.

The Papal States

Bologna

Ravenna

Imola
Faenza
Forli •Cervia
Cesena
Rimini

R
O
M
A
G
N
A

Pesaro
Fano

Pisa

Florence

Urbino

Senigallia

Arno R.

Ancona

Arezzo

Città di Castello

T
H
E

M
A
R
C
H
E
S

Siena

L. Trasimeno
Perugia

Assisi

Camerino

Fermo

•Città di Pieve

Piombino

UMBRIA

Ascoli

Grosseto

Acquapendente
Orvieto
•Todi
Spoleto

Montefiascone
•Viterbo

Tiber R.

SABINA

Pescara

L. Bracciano

Civitavecchia
Bracciano

Tivoli

Rome

Subiaco

Ostia

CAMPAGNA
&
MARITTIMA

Ceprano

0 10 20 30 40 50 miles

Terracina

C. Brandon Schmitt 1979

VII

OF NEW PRINCIPATES WHICH BY THE ARMS OF OTHERS AND FORTUNE ARE ACQUIRED*

Those who are private men and become princes only by fortune, do so with little toil, but with much [toil] do they maintain themselves; and they do not have any difficulties on the way because they fly there; but all the difficulties arise after they are placed. And of such kind are those who are given a state either because of money or because of the grace of him who gives it: as happened to many in Greece, in the cities of Ionia and the Hellespont where princes were made by Darius,[1] so that they might keep it [the state] for his security and glory; and as was done again by those emperors who, from private [station], attained to the imperium by corruption of the soldiers.[2]

These stand simply on the will and the fortune of him who has granted it to them; but these two things are most volatile and unstable: they do not, and cannot keep that station. They do not, because unless a man is of great intelligence and virtue, it is not reasonable [to expect] that he should know how to command, having always lived in private fortune; they cannot, because they do not have the forces which could be faithful and friendly to them. Moreover, states that immediately come to one, like all the

*De Principatibus Novis Qui Alienis Armis et Fortuna Acquirantur

other things of nature that are born and grow quickly, cannot establish their roots with all the corresponding branches; in such a mode the first adverse weather extinguishes them — unless, as has been said, those who suddenly become princes are already of a virtue equal to that which fortune has thrown in their laps, and they know immediately how to prepare themselves to preserve it, and those foundations which others have made before they became princes, they afterwards make.

I wish with regard to these two said modes of becoming a prince — either by virtue or by fortune — to adduce two examples within living memory: Francesco Sforza³ and Cesare Borgia. Francesco, by proper means and with his own great virtue, became Duke of Milan from a private [station]; and that which he had with a thousand pains acquired, he with little toil maintained. On the other hand, Cesare Borgia, whom the vulgar called Duke Valentino,⁴ acquired the state with his father's fortune, and with the same he lost it; notwithstanding that he used every means, and that he did all those things which ought to be done by a prudent and virtuous man to establish his roots in those states that the arms and fortune of others had granted to him. For he who does not first make his foundations, as was said above, might yet be able to make them afterwards, by [means of] a very great virtue; although it might have to be done with hardship to the architect and danger to the edifice. If, then, one considers all the Duke's progresses, he will see that he had made for himself great foundations for future power. I judge these not superfluous to discuss, because I do not know what better precepts there could be for me to give to a new prince than the example of his actions. And if these orders of his did not profit him, it was not his fault, because this [failure to profit] arose from the extraordinary and extreme malignity of fortune.

Alexander VI had many difficulties, present and future, in wishing to make the Duke, his son, great.⁵ First, he saw no way whereby he might be able to make him the lord of any state except that which was already a state of the Church. And if he wished to take that which belonged to the Church, he knew that the Duke of Milan and the Venetians would never consent to it, because Faenza and Rimini were already under the protection of the Venetians.[6] Besides, he saw that the arms of Italy, and in particular those which could have served him, were in the hands of those who had cause to fear the greatness of the Pope, and therefore he could not trust them — all of these arms were in the [hands of the] Orsini and the Colonnas and their followers.[7] It was necessary, then, that he upset these orders and [that he put into] disorder the states of all these so that he might, in security, become the lord of part of them. This was easy for he found that the Venetians, moved by other causes, had decided to let the French enter Italy again; which entrance he not only did not oppose, but made most easy by resolving the question of King Louis' previous marriage.

The King then passed into Italy with the aid of the Venetians and the consent of Alexander; and he was no sooner in Milan than the Pope had troops from him for the enterprise of the Romagna; which was granted to him because of the reputation of the King.[8] The Duke acquired, then, the Romagna; and with the Colonnas beaten down, he wanted to keep that [acquisition] and proceed further ahead. Two things impeded him: one, his arms, which did not seem to be faithful to him; the other, the will of France — that is to say, that the Orsini arms, which he was using, might fail him, and might not only impede his acquiring [more] but might take away his acquisitions; and that the King might also do the same. [His suspicions] of the Orsini were verified when, after the conquest of Faenza, he assaulted Bologna — there he saw them go coldly to that assault; and of the King, he knew his mind when, having taken the Duchy of Urbino, he assaulted Tuscany, from which enterprise the King made him desist.[9] Whereupon the Duke resolved to depend no longer on the arms and fortune of others.

First, he weakened the Orsini and Colonna factions in Rome; for he gained all [their] adherents who were of the Roman nobility, by making them his gentlemen and paying them large allowances; and he honored them according to their qualities, with commands and ministries; in such a mode that in a few months their affections for their factions were quite extinguished in their minds, and all were turned to the Duke. After this, he waited for an occasion to extinguish the chieftains of the Orsini, having already dispersed the house of Colonna — a good one came to him, and he used it even better. For the Orsini, perceiving too late that the Duke's greatness and that of the Church was their ruin, called a diet at Magione, in Perugia;[10] whence arose the rebellion of Urbino and the tumults of the Romagna and infinite dangers for the Duke; all of which he overcame with the aid of the French.

And having regained his reputation, trusting neither in the French nor in any other outside forces, so that he need not test them, he turned to deceptions. And he knew so well how to dissimulate his mind that the Orsini themselves, through Signor Paulo, were reconciled to him. The Duke forgot not one reason [or duty] of office [in attempting] to assure [Signor Paulo], giving him money, clothes and horses; such that their simplicity conducted them to Sinigaglia into his hands.[11] Having thus extinguished these chieftains, and reduced their partisans into his friends, the Duke sufficiently had in range good foundations for his power, having all the Romagna with the Duchy of Urbino; but principally he appeared to have acquired the friendship of the Romagna, gaining to himself all its people as they began to taste the good that was to be theirs.

And because this part is worthy of notice and of imitation by others, I do not want to omit it. The Duke, having taken the Romagna, found it commanded by impotent lords who had been quicker to despoil their subjects than to correct them, and who gave them matter for disunion, not for union. As the province was full of robberies, of factional quarrels, and of every other reason for arrogance; he judged it necessary, wishing to reduce [that province] to peace and obedience under the princely arm, to give them good government. So that he placed there Messer Remirro de Orco, a cruel and expeditious man, to whom he gave the fullest power. That man, in a little time, and with very great reputation, reduced it to peace and unity. The Duke then judged that such excessive authority was not necessary, because he did not doubt that it would arouse hatred; and he set up a civil judiciary, in which every city had its own advocate, in the midst of that province, with a most excellent president. And because he knew that the past severities had generated some hatred, in order to purge the minds of that people and to gain them all to himself, he wished to show that if any cruelty had been done, it had not come from him, but from the harsh nature of his minister. And he found an occasion: he had him placed one morning in the piazza in Cesena in two pieces, with a piece of wood and a bloody knife alongside.[12] The ferocity of that spectacle left the people at the same time satisfied and stupefied.

But let us return to where we left off. I say that the Duke, finding himself powerful enough and in part secured against present dangers — being armed in his own mode and having in good part extinguished those arms which, because near, could harm him — wishing to proceed with acquisition, there remained the King of France for his consideration. For he knew that the King, who was late to realize his error, would not support him. Because of this he began to look for new friends, and he temporized with France with respect to the French expedition to the Kingdom of Naples against the Spanish, who were then besieging Gaeta. And he was of a mind to assure himself of them. He would quickly have succeeded in doing so, had Alexander lived.

And this was how he managed present things.

But as to the future, he had to doubt, first of all, whether a new successor to the Church would be friendly to him; and therefore, that he might seek to take away that which Alexander had given to him. He thought of securing himself in four modes: first, by extinguishing all the blood of those lords that he had dispossessed, in order to take that opportunity away from the Pope; secondly, by gaining to himself all the gentlemen of Rome, as has been said, to hold the Pope in check; thirdly, to reduce further the College of Cardinals to his power; fourthly, to acquire such imperium before the Pope's death, that he could resist the first attack [of his enemies]. Of these four things, at the death of Alexander, he had conducted three; the fourth he had almost under his conduct.[13] Of the dispossessed lords, he killed as many as he possibly could, and very few saved themselves; he had gained the Roman gentlemen, and of the College he had the greatest part; and, as to new acquisition, he had planned to become the lord of Tuscany. He already possessed Perugia and Piombino, and he had taken Pisa under his protection.

And since he no longer needed to have respect for France — he no longer needed to do so, for the French had already been dispossessed of the Kingdom [of Naples] by the Spanish in such a way that each of these was necessitated to compete for his friendship — he would have leaped into Pisa. After this, Lucca and Siena would have quickly surrendered, partly from envy of the Florentines, partly from fear; and the Florentines would have had no remedy. Had he succeeded in this (as he was in the year that Alexander died), he would have acquired such forces and such reputation that he could have stood up by himself, and he would no longer have depended on the fortune and forces of others, but on his own power and virtue. But Alexander died five years after he had begun to draw forth the sword.[14] He left Cesare with the state of the Romagna alone consolidated, with all the others up in the air, [caught] between two very powerful enemy armies, and sick unto death.

And there was in the Duke such ferocity and such virtue, and he knew so well how men have to be gained or lost, and so sound were the foundations which he laid in so little time, that, had those armies not been on his back, or had he been healthy, he would have stood up to every difficulty. And one can see that his foundations were well-laid: for the Romagna waited for him more than a month; in Rome, though but half-alive, he was safe, and although the Baglioni, the Vitelli, and the Orsini came to Rome, none followed them against him; and if he was not able to make someone whom he wanted pope, at least it would not be someone whom he did not want. But, if he had been healthy on the death of Alexander, everything would have been easy for him. And he told me, on the day that Julius II was made pope, that he had thought on all which could arise from his father's death, and that he had found a remedy for everything except that he had never thought that when his father was at the point of death that he would also be close to death.[15]

Summing up all the actions of the Duke, I would not know how to find fault with him. On the contrary; it seems to me he [ought to be] set up, as I have done, to be imitated by all those who by fortune and with the arms of others have ascended to imperium. For having a great mind and high intentions, he could not govern otherwise; and only the brief life of Alexander and his own illness thwarted his plans. Whoever, then, judges it necessary in his new principate to assure himself of his enemies, to gain to himself friends, to conquer either by force or by fraud, to make himself loved and feared by the people, followed and revered by the soldiers, to extinguish those who can or must harm you,[16] to innovate the ancient orders with new modes, to be severe and gracious, magnanimous and liberal, to extinguish the unfaithful militia and create a new one, to maintain the friendship of kings and princes in such a mode that they must benefit you graciously or offend you with respect, one cannot find fresher examples than the actions of that man.

One can accuse him only of creating Julius pontiff, in which he made a bad choice; for, as has been said, being unable to make a pope in his own mode, he could have kept anyone from being made pope; and he should never have consented to the papacy of those cardinals whom he had harmed or who, once made pope, would have cause to fear him. For men do harm either from fear or from hate. Those whom he had offended were, among others, San Piero ad Vincula, Colonna, San Giorgio, Ascanio;[17] all the others, once they were made pope, would have cause to fear him, except Rouen and the Spaniards; the latter because of their relationship to him and their obligations; the former because of power, having conjoined with him the kingdom of France. Therefore, the Duke, before everything else, ought to have created a Spaniard as pope, and not being able to do so, he ought to have consented to Rouen's being [made pope] and not San Piero ad Vincula. And whoever believes that great personages are made to forget old injuries by new benefits deceives himself. The Duke erred, then, in this election; and this was the cause of his ultimate ruin.

Notes

1. Darius I (521-486 B.C.).

2. See below, Ch. XIX. See also Montesquieu, *Greatness of the Romans,* Ch. XVI.

3. For Francesco Sforza, see above Ch. I, n. 6. See also Ch. XII below.

4. Cesare Borgia (1476-1507) was called "Il Valentino" because, when he resigned his position as a cardinal, he was made Duke of Valence in France by Louis XII. Since he had been Bishop of Valencia, Spain, the French title was an appropriate one, indicating his home city. The first Borgia pope, Calixtus III, had been also popularly called "Il Valentino," because he was Bishop of Valencia.

The events of 1494-1504, which concern the enterprises of the Borgias, are narrated in two poems by Machiavelli, *The Decen-*

nali. See Machiavelli, *The Chief Works and Others,* trans. Allan Gilbert (Durham, N.C.: Duke University Press, 1965), III, pp. 1444-1462. Cited hereafter as *Chief Works.*

5. See Ch. III, n.22, above.

6. The Papal States in the late 15th century included in western and central Italy, Velletri, Rome, Ostia, Viterbo, Orvieto, Perugia, and Urbino. In the Romagna and the Marches were Ancona, Senigallia, Fano, Pesaro, Rimini, Cesena, Forlì, Faenza, Imola; and, finally, in the north, were Bologna and Ferrara. In practice, most of these cities were ruled by *signori*, in semi-independence or independence of the Pope.

7. The Orsini and the Colonnas, two of the greatest families of the Roman nobility, had struggled with each other for two centuries for the control of Rome and the papacy. The Orsini had been enemies of the Borgias from the beginning, and a war against them was waged by Alexander VI in 1496-97.

8. The reference here is to the enterprise of the Romagna, and not to the troops. Thus the meaning is that Alexander and Cesare were permitted to enter the Romagna because of the reputation of the King of France.

9. "He" refers throughout to the Duke, Cesare Borgia.

10. This council of war met October 9, 1502, to seek means to stop Cesare Borgia. Those attending included Bentivogli (Bologna), the Orsini, Baglioni (Perugia), Pandolfo Petrucci (Siena), Vitelozzo Vitelli (Città di Castello), and Oliverotto Euffreducci da Fermo among others.

11. These *condottieri* were called to a meeting with Cesare on December 31, 1502, and were there arrested by him. Vitelli and Oliverotto were strangled the next morning (see Ch. VIII). The Orsini were subsequently arrested in Rome, and a siege of the Orsini strongholds in the Campagna, Ceri and Bracciano followed. Machiavelli narrates these events in "A Description of the

Method Used by Duke Valentino in Killing Vitellozo Vitelli, Oliverotto da Fermo, and Others," *Chief Works*, I, pp. 163-169. Sinigaglia is the modern Senigallia.

12. Remirro de Orco (Don Ramiro de Lorqua), one of Cesare Borgia's Spanish captains and his major-domo, was named governor of the Romagna in 1501. (I have preserved the spelling Machiavelli uses.) He was executed December 26, 1502. The mode of execution, as Machiavelli says, was meant to satisfy and stupefy the people. It is a "rare example" of which much will be said (see Ch. XXI, n. 1, below). The bloody knife and the piece of wood add touches of mystery which will necessarily evoke much wonder.

13. *ne aveva condotte tu—ne aveva per condotta* — A *condotta* is the contract with a mercenary captain and his company of soldiers. See Ch. XII, n. 23, below. Here, "almost under [his] conduct," is to be understood as "he had almost brought it to its completion."

14. It is Alexander who draws the sword and not Cesare. See Ch. XI, n. 8, below.

15. Alexander and Cesare both fell ill in August, 1503. The two armies on his back were the French at Viterbo, and the Spanish, who were moving toward Rome from Naples. Cesare did not however die until 1507, when he was killed in a skirmish fighting for the King of Navarre, his brother-in-law.

16. On the shift from the third to the second person familiar, see Ch. VI, n. 1, above.

17. Giuliano della Rovere (Pope Julius II), was the titular cardinal of the Church of San Pietro in Vincoli in Rome; the others were the Cardinal Giovanni Colonna; Raffaele Riario, the titular cardinal of the Church of San Giorgio; and the Cardinal Ascanio Sforza. The Cardinal of Rouen was Georges d'Amboise (see Ch. III, above).

VIII

OF THOSE WHO THROUGH WICKEDNESSES
ATTAIN TO THE PRINCIPATE*

But because one rises from a private [station] and becomes a prince in still two more modes, neither of which is wholly attributable to fortune or to virtue, it does not seem to me that I should omit them, even though it is possible to reason on one of them at more length in a treatise on republics.[1] These two modes are: when one ascends to the principate by some wicked and nefarious way, or when a private citizen, by the favor of his other fellow citizens, becomes the prince of his fatherland. And what is said of the first mode will be demonstrated with two examples, one ancient, the other modern, without entering otherwise into the merits of such a [mode], because I judge it sufficient, for whoever would find it necessary, to imitate them.

Agathocles, the Sicilian, not only from a private, but from a low and abject fortune, became king of Syracuse.[2] That man, who was born of a potter, always led a wicked life at every stage; nevertheless, he accompanied his wickednesses with such virtue of mind and body that, when he joined the militia, he rose through the ranks and became the praetor of Syracuse. Once established in that rank, he determined to become prince and to hold with

De His Qui Per Scelera ad Principatum Pervenere

51

violence and without obligation to others, that which by agreement had been conceded to him. And having given intelligence of his plan to Hamilcar, the Carthaginian (who was fighting with his armies in Sicily), he assembled the people and the Senate of Syracuse, as if to deliberate on things pertinent to the republic; and, upon a given signal, he had his soldiers kill all the senators and the richest of the people; once they were dead, he seized and held the principate of that city without any civil controversy. And although he was twice broken in the field by the Carthaginians and ultimately besieged, he was able not only to defend his city but, leaving part of his troops to defend against siege, he assaulted Africa with the others, and in a short time not only liberated Syracuse from the siege but drove the Carthaginians into extreme necessity: and they were necessitated to come to an agreement with him — they had to be satisfied with the possession of Africa and leave Sicily to Agathocles.

Whoever might consider then the actions and life of that man will see nothing or little which can be attributed to fortune; for that which he gained, as was said above, was not through the favor of anyone, but by his ascent through the ranks of the militia with a thousand hardships and dangers — which principate he then, moreover, maintained with many spirited and dangerous decisions. Still, one cannot call it virtue to kill his fellow citizens, to betray his friends, to be without faith, without pity, without religion; which modes enabled him to acquire imperium, but not glory.[3] For if one considers the virtue of Agathocles in entering into and escaping from dangers, and the greatness of his mind in standing up to and overcoming adverse things, one does not see why he should have to be judged inferior to any of the most excellent captains;[4] nevertheless, his brutal cruelty and inhumanity and his infinite wickednesses do not allow that he be among the most excellent celebrated men. One cannot then attribute to fortune or to virtue that which, without the one or the other, was accomplished by him.

In our times, in the reign of Alexander VI, Liverotto of Fermo[5] having been left fatherless a few years earlier, while still little, was raised by one of his maternal uncles, a man named Giovanni Fogliani, and in the beginning of his youth he was apprenticed to soldier under Paulo Vitelli,[6] so that replete with that discipline, he might attain some excellent rank in the militia. Afterwards, when Paulo was dead, he soldiered under Vitellozo, Paulo's brother; and in a very short time, by being ingenious, and vigorous in his person and mind, he became the first man of his militia. But since it seemed to him a·servile thing to be under others, he thought, with the aid of some citizens of Fermo to whom servitude was dearer than the liberty of their fatherland and with the favor of the Vitelli, to seize Fermo. He wrote to Giovanni Fogliani [explaining] how, having been many years away from home, he wanted to return to see him and his city and to acknowledge in some part his patrimony. And because he had not worn himself out in labor other than to acquire honor, in order that his fellow citizens would see that he had not spent the time in vain, he wanted to return honorably, accompanied by one hundred horse of his friends and servants; and he prayed [that Fogliani] be pleased to order that the Firmani might receive him honorably; and that would give honor not only to him [Giovanni], but also to himself, since he had been his pupil.

Giovanni, therefore, did not fail in any due office toward his nephew: he made the Firmani receive him honorably. Liverotto lodged in his own houses[7] where he waited to order secretly that which was necessary for his future wickedness. After some days had passed he gave a most solemn banquet to which he invited Giovanni Fogliani and all the first men of Fermo. And when the meal and the other entertainments that are usual at all such banquets were over, Liverotto, with art, moved certain serious arguments, speaking of the greatness of Pope Alexander and of his son, Cesare, and of their enterprises. Giovanni and the others responding to these arguments, he suddenly rose up, saying these were things which one ought to speak of in a more secret place. So he retired into a room, where Giovanni and all the other citizens followed him. They were no sooner seated than soldiers came out from secret places and killed Giovanni and all the others.

After that homicide, Liverotto mounted a horse, and, coursing the town, besieged the supreme magistrate in the palace; so that from fear they were constrained to obey him and to form a government of which he was made prince. Since all those were dead who would have been malcontented and able to harm him, he strengthened himself with new civil and military orders, in such a mode that, in the year that he held the principate, not only was he safe in the city of Fermo, but all his neighbors feared him. And to overthrow him would have been as difficult as overthrowing Agathocles, had he not let himself be deceived by Cesare Borgia, when at Sinigaglia, as has been said above,[8] Cesare took the Orsini and Vitelli; where, having also been taken by him, one year after he had committed the parricide, he was, together with Vitellozo who had been his teacher in virtue and wickednesses, strangled.

One might doubt whence it arose that Agathocles and others like him, after infinite treacheries and cruelties, could long live safe in their fatherland and defend themselves against external enemies, and yet never have the citizens conspire against them, since there have been many others who have not been able to maintain the state through cruelty even in peaceful times, not to mention the dubious times of war. I believe that this comes to pass from cruelty badly used or well used. Well used one is able to call those [cruelties] (if one may lawfully call the bad good) which are done at one stroke for the necessity of securing oneself, and which are afterwards not continued within, but converted to the greatest possible utility of the subjects. Badly used are those which, even though they are at the beginning few, soon increase with time rather than become extinguished. Those who observe the first mode are able to have some remedy for their state with God and with men[9] as did Agathocles; as for the others, it is impossible that they maintain themselves.

Whence it is to be noted that in taking a state, the occupier ought to reason out all those offenses that are necessary for him to do; and do them all at one stroke in order not to have to renew them daily. He is thus able, by not innovating them, to assure men and gain them to himself by benefiting them. Whoever does otherwise, either from timidity or bad counsel, is always necessitated to hold knife in hand; nor can he ever rely on his subjects, since they are unable, because of fresh and continuous injuries, to assure themselves of him. For all the injuries ought to be done all together, for being tasted less, they offend less. The benefits ought to be done little by little, so that they may be tasted better. And a prince ought, above all, to live with his subjects in such a mode that no one accident, either bad or good, will make him vary [his policy]. For necessity coming with adverse times, you[10] cannot be in time with the bad, nor will the good that you do help you, because it is judged to be forced, and you do not know any thanks.

Notes

1. See Machiavelli's *Discourses,* III, passim.

2. Agathocles (361-289 B.C.). He overthrew the oligarchs in 317. See also *Discourses* II.12, 13: III.6.

3. See the discussion of *virtù* in the Introduction.

4. *capitano* — a captain is one who is professed in the art of warfare (Ch. XIV, below), that is, a man capable of commanding men, and possessing the strategic art. That the prince must be a captain is explicitly stated in Ch. XII, below. Since Machiavelli claims to be able to educate princes in the art of war (see Ch. XIV, below) and he writes a book called *The Art of War,* one wonders if he himself is a captain.

5. Oliverotto Euffreducci da Fermo. See Ch. VII, nn. 10 and 11, above. He took Fermo in December, 1501.

6. Paulo Vitelli was one of the most reputed of the *condottieri*. He commanded the Florentine army in the war against Pisa, was suspected of treason, condemned to death, and beheaded in 1499.

7. He owned several houses in the city which he and his entourage occupied.

8. See Ch. VII, n. 11, above.

9. The belief in cruelty well-used is quite literally Machiavelli's credo. Such a belief permits one, as he says here, to redeem oneself, reconciling one with man and God. See Ch. XIII, n. 15 and Ch. XVII, n. 1, below.

10. The second person familiar is used. See Ch. VI, n.1, above.

IX

OF THE CIVIL PRINCIPATE*

But coming to the other part, when a private citizen neither by wickedness nor other intolerable violence, but with the favor of his fellow citizens, becomes prince of his fatherland (which one can call a civil principate; nor is it necessary to attain it either wholly through virtue or wholly through fortune, but more nearly [through] a fortunate astuteness), I say that that one ascends to this principate either with the favor of the people or with that of the great. For in every city these two different humors are to be found: and it comes of this that the people desire not to be commanded or oppressed by the great, and the great desire to command and to oppress the people; and from these two different appetites one of three effects issues in the cities — either a principate, liberty, or license.

The principate is established either by the people or by the great, according to whether one or the other of these parties has the occasion. For the great, when they see they are not able to resist the people, begin turning to the reputation of one of their own, making him prince, so they may, under his shadow, give vent to their appetite. The people also, when they see that they are not

*De Principatu Civili

able to resist the great, turn to the reputation of one, and make him a prince, in order to be defended with his authority. He who comes to the principate with the aid of the great maintains himself with more difficulty than the one who attains to it with the aid of the people — for he finds himself prince with many around him who opine themselves his equals, and because of this he cannot command or manage them in his own mode.

But he who arrives at the principate with the popular favor finds himself alone, and there will be no one or very few around him who are not prepared to obey Besides this, one cannot with honesty satisfy the great without injuring others, but one can well do that with the people.[1] For the end of the people is more honest than that of the great, the latter wanting to oppress, the former not to be oppressed. Moreover, with the people as enemies, a prince is never able to assure himself of them, because they are many. He is able to assure himself of the great because they are few. The worst that a prince can expect from a people who are his enemies is to be abandoned by them; with the great as his enemies, he must not only fear being abandoned, but also fear their coming against him — for they have more foresight, are more astute, and always take steps to save themselves in time, and they seek the gratitude of the one they hope might win. The prince is also necessitated to live always with the same people; but he can do very well without the same great ones; because he can make and unmake them every day, and take away and give, at his disposal, their reputation.

And in order better to clarify this part, I say that one ought to consider the great principally in two modes: they either govern themselves in their proceedings in such a mode that they are wholly obligated to your[2] fortune, or they do not. Those who are so obligated and who are not rapacious ought to be honored and loved; those who are not obligated have to be examined in two modes. If they keep themselves from you because of pusillanimity and a natural lack of spirit,[3] then you should have them serve you, especially those who are of good counsel; because in prosperity they bring you honor, and in adversity you need not fear them. But if they do not obligate themselves out of art and because of ambition, it is a sign that they are thinking more of themselves than of you; and it is these whom the prince should watch and fear as if they were discovered enemies, because they will always, in adversity, help to ruin him.

One who becomes prince by means of the favor of the people ought, therefore, to keep them his friends. This is made easy for him for they ask of him only that they be not oppressed. But one who becomes prince with the favor of the great, against the people, ought above all things to gain the people to himself; which is easily done when he undertakes their protection. And since men, when good comes from one from whom they believe they will have evil, are more obligated to their benefactor, the people are then immediately more well-disposed to him than if he had been conducted to the principate with their own favor. And the prince may gain [the people] in many modes; but because these [modes] vary according to the subject, a certain rule cannot be given, and they will therefore be omitted.

I shall conclude only that it is necessary for a prince to have the people friendly; otherwise, in adversity, he does not have a remedy. Nabis, prince of the Spartans,[4] sustained the siege of the whole of Greece and one of the most victorious of Roman armies, and defended his fatherland and his state against them. When the danger appeared, one thing alone sufficed him, that he assure himself of the few; if he had had the people as his enemies, this would not have been enough. And let no one contradict my opinion with that trite proverb, that he who founds on the people, founds on mud; for that is true if a private citizen lays his foundation there and gives himself to understand that the people will rescue him if he is oppressed by enemies or by the magistrates (in this case one could often find himself deceived, as were the Gracchi in Rome[5] and Messer Giorgio Scali[6] in Florence). But a

59

prince who founds [on the people], who is able to command, and is a man of heart, is not dismayed in adversity, and if he does not lack other preparations, and if with his mind and his orders he animates the whole, he will never find himself deceived by them — and he will see that he has laid for himself good foundations.

Usually these principates are put in danger when they are in transition from a civil order[7] to an absolute one. For such princes either take command themselves or appoint magistrates. In the latter case, their place is weaker and more dangerous, because they are wholly dependent upon the will of those citizens who are appointed magistrates; for these, especially in adverse times, can with great facility take away the state, either by opposition or disobedience. And the prince cannot, in the midst of dangers, take absolute authority in time, because the citizens and subjects who usually obey the magistrates are not, in these shoals, going to obey him; and there will always in dubious times be a dearth of those whom he can trust. For such a prince cannot found himself on what he sees in quiet times, when the citizens have need of the state; for then everyone runs, everyone promises, and everyone wants to die for him, when death is far off; but in adverse times, when the state has need of citizens, then few of them are to be found. And so much the more is this experience dangerous, since one cannot have it more than once. Therefore a wise prince ought to think of a mode whereby his citizens, always and in every quality of time, have need of the state and of him; and then they will always be faithful to him.

Notes

1. On the nature of the people, that is, the many, see *Discourses* I. passim; II.27, 30; III.6, 12, 19-23, 28-31, 34. Cf. I.11, III.8.

2. The second person familiar is used.

3. *animo* — See the Epistle Dedicatory, n. 8, above.

4. Nabis, tyrant of Sparta from 205 to 192 B.C. Machiavelli does not mention his assassination, the result of an Aetolian conspiracy, in 192. See *Discourses*, III.6; I.10, 40. He was attacked by Philopoemen and Flamininus in 193.

5. The Gracchi, Tiberius and Gaius Sempronius sought to reform the Roman constitution by increasing the popular and knightly power against the Senatorial nobility. Tiberius was murdered by a Senatorial gang in 133 B.C. Gaius had one of his slaves kill him in 121 B.C., to avoid being taken by his enemies. The Gracchi, according to Machiavelli, were imprudent in seeking radically to restore republican ways when evil ways had become habitual. See *Discourses*, I.37, 4 and 6.

6. Giorgio Scali was one of the heads of a popular rebellion in Florence which was called the Tumult of the Ciompi (1378). The Ciompi were unincorporated laborers in the wool industry and formed the most numerous and powerful of the minor Arts, that is, of the trades which employed the lowest of the people, the "plebeians" as Machiavelli called them. A popular government was established and the oligarchical party, the Guelfs, were either oppressed or exiled. Scali, together with some others, proved however to be too democratic or plebeian even for the popular government and he was beheaded. See the *Florentine Histories*, III.1-20. See Ch. XII, n. 19, below.

7. Note that the "civil order" is one in which there is liberty. Liberty, as was implied above, is to be found in the city (see Ch. V, n. 2, above).

X

IN WHAT MODE THE STRENGTHS OF ALL PRINCIPATES OUGHT TO BE WEIGHED*

In examining the qualities of these principates, it is requisite to have another consideration: that is, whether a prince has such state[1] that if he finds himself in need, he can himself stand up by his own means, or whether he finds it always necessary to be defended by others. In order better to clarify this part, I say that I judge those [princes] able to stand up by their own means, who can, either by abundance of men or of money, put together a proper army and make a day of it[2] with anyone who attacks them. And I therefore judge those who cannot appear in the field against the enemy, but are necessitated to take refuge inside their walls and guard them, as always having necessity of others. The first case has been discussed; what is further requisite will be said in the future. In the second case, nothing can be said, except to encourage such princes to fortify and provide for their town[3] and not take any account of the countryside. And whoever fortifies well his own town, and if he has managed the other matters respecting the government of his subjects according to what has been said above, and will be said below, he will always be attacked with great caution; for men are always hostile to enterprises wherein they see difficulties, and they will see that it is not easy to

*Quomodo Omnium Principatuum Vires Perpendi Debeant

attack someone who has kept his town strong and who is not hated by the people.

The cities of Germany are free to the highest degree; they have little countryside, and they obey the Emperor when they want to; they fear neither him nor any other neighboring power, for they are fortified in such a mode that everyone thinks that conquering them would be tedious and difficult. For they all possess the requisite moats and walls; they have adequate artillery; they always keep a year's drink, food and fuel in the public larders; and besides this, so that the plebs may be fed without loss to the public, they always keep on hand a common fund sufficient for one year, whereby they can give them work in those employments which are the nerve and the life of the city and in those industries which feed the people. They still hold military exercises in repute, and have many ordinances to maintain them.[4]

A prince, then, who has a strong city and who does not make himself hated, cannot be attacked; and if someone were to attack him, that [attacker] would have to retreat in shame; for the things of the world are so variable, that it is almost impossible that one could stand one year idle and encamped with his army. And if someone might reply: if the people have their possessions outside and see them burning, they will not have patience; and the long siege and the love of their own will make them forget the prince, I respond that a powerful and spirited prince will always overcome these difficulties — now giving his subjects hope that the evil might not last long, now [making them] fear the cruelty of the enemy, now securing himself with dexterity against those who seem too bold. Besides this, it would seem reasonable that the enemy would burn and ruin the countryside immediately upon their arrival, and it is at these times that the minds of men are still hot and willing for the defense;[5] and therefore so much the less ought the prince doubt, for afterwards, whichever day men's minds turn cold, the damage will already have been done, the evils will have been received, and there is no more remedy: and now even more will they unite with their prince, since it appears that he has an obligation toward them, their houses having been burned and their possessions ruined for his defense. And the nature of men is such that they obligate themselves to another as much for the benefits they give as for those they receive. Wherefore, if one will consider all these things well, it will not be difficult for a prudent prince first to keep, and later, to hold firm the minds of the citizens during a siege when they lack neither the means of life nor the means to defend themselves.

Notes

1. On the use of the word "state," see Ch. I, n. 3, above.

2. *fare una giornata* — "to make a day of it." As Machiavelli explains, in Discourses II.17, beg., the *zuffe campali,* or battles in the open country, are called by the French *giornate* (days), and by the Italians *fatti d'arme* (feats of arms).

3. *terra* — the town; that is, the area within the walls.

4. See also *"Rapporto delle cose della Magna. Fatto questo di 17 giugno 1508,"* in *Tutte le Opere* (Florence: Sansoni, 1971), p. 66; and the *"Ritratto delle cose della Magna," Tutte le Opere,* ed. by Flora and Cordié, I, pp. 697-702. In the *"Ritratto"* (p. 697) Machiavelli says of Germany:

> Of the power of Germany no one ought to doubt, because of the abundance of men, of wealth and of arms . . . And they have in this a very fine [*bellissimo*] law, for they always have in common food and drink and fuel for one year: thus they are able to work their industries, by being able in a siege, to feed the plebs and those who live by [the strength of] their arms for one whole year without loss. They do not spend anything on soldiers, because they exercise and arm their own men; and on festival days, instead of games, these men exercise with the petronel [carbine or horse-pistol], the pike, and with one or the other of such arms, playing among themselves for honors and such, and for that which among themselves they take pleasure. On salaries and other things they spend little: such that every community is to be found rich in public wealth.

On Germany (and the Swiss), see *Discourses,* I.12, 55; II. Preface, 4, 12, 18, 19; III.43. The term "della Magna" is a form of "Allemagna."

5. One is reminded of Pericles' strategy in the Peloponnesian War. See Thucydides, *Peloponnesian War,* II. 13-23, 65.

XI

OF ECCLESIASTICAL PRINCIPATES*

There only remains, at present, to reason of ecclesiastical principates,[1] whose difficulties all arise before they are possessed; for they are acquired either by virtue or fortune, and are maintained without either; for these are sustained by the ancient orders of religion, which have been so powerful and are of such quality, that they keep their princes in state, in whatever mode they proceed and live. These alone have states which they do not defend and subjects which they do not govern; and these states, by not being defended, are never taken away and the subjects, by not being governed, never care — they never think of alienating themselves from their princes, nor could they do so if they thought of it. Only these princes, then, are secure and happy.

But since these stand by a superior cause, the superiority of which [causes] the human mind cannot grasp,[2] I shall leave off speaking of them; and since they are exalted and maintained by God, it would be the office of a presumptuous and bold man to discuss them. Nevertheless, if someone demanded of me how it came to be that the Church came to such greatness in temporal [affairs], since one finds that prior to Alexander, the Italian po-

*De Principatibus Ecclesiasticis

66

tentates (and not only those who are called potentates, but every baron and lord, no matter how petty) so little esteemed her in the temporal, and now a king of France trembles before her and she has been able to drive him from Italy and ruin the Venetians — even though all this is well known, it does not seem to me superfluous to recall a good part of it to memory.

Before Charles, King of France,[3] passed into Italy, this province was under the imperium of the Pope, the Venetians, the King of Naples, the Duke of Milan, and the Florentines.[4] These potentates had to have two principal cares: one, that a foreigner not enter Italy with arms; the other, that no one among themselves seize more state.[5] Those of whom they had to take the most care were the Pope and the Venetians. And to restrain the Venetians, all the others had to unite, as occurred in the defense of Ferrara. The Roman barons served to keep the Pope down, and since they were divided into two factions, the Orsini and Colonnas, there was always a cause of disruptions between them. But standing with arms in hand before the eyes of the pontiff, they kept the pontificate weak and infirm. And although a spirited pope rose up at times, like Sixtus,[6] yet neither fortune nor wisdom could ever release him from these incommodities. And the brevity of their lives was the cause; for in the ten years which is, on the average, the length of a pope's reign, he might, with difficulty, put down one of the factions; and if, for instance, one had almost extinguished the Colonnas, another pope rose up hostile to the Orsini — that would permit the Colonnas to recover, and the Orsini would not be in time to extinguish [them].[7] This was what made the temporal forces of the Pope to be so little esteemed in Italy.

Then Alexander VI rose up who, of all pontiffs that have ever been, showed how much a pope with money and with forces could prevail. With Duke Valentino as his instrument[8] and the passage of the French [into Italy] as the occasion, he did all those things which I have discussed above with respect to the actions of the Duke. Although his intent might not have been to make the

Church great (but rather the Duke), what he did, nevertheless, gave rise to the greatness of the Church. And with Alexander's death, and the extinction of the Duke, the Church became heir to all his toils. Then came Pope Julius, and he found the Church great; for she now possessed all of the Romagna; the barons of Rome were extinguished and the blows struck by Alexander had annihilated the factions; and, moreover, he also found the way open to a mode of accumulating money which previous to Alexander had never been used.[9]

These things Julius not only continued but increased; he thought to gain Bologna for himself and to extinguish the Venetians, and chase the French out of Italy. He succeeded in all these enterprises; and much to his praise, all these things were done to increase the Church and not any private [man].[10] He also kept the Orsini and Colonna factions within the same limits in which he found them; and although there were some leaders among them who wanted from time to time to rebel, two things yet restrained them: one, the greatness of the Church, which dismayed them; the other, not having cardinals of their own, for the [cardinals] are the origin of the tumults among [the Roman factions]. Whenever they have cardinals, these factions will never remain quiet, for these [cardinals] nourish factions in Rome and elsewhere, and the barons are then forced to defend them. Thus from the ambitions of the prelates arise all the discords and tumults among the barons. His Holiness Pope Leo, then, found this pontificate most powerful; and, one hopes that if his predecessors made her great with arms, he, with his goodness and his infinite other virtues, will make her very great and venerated.

Notes

1. See also the *Discourses*, I.11, 12; II. Preface, 2, 5; III.1. Cf. Ch. XIX, n. 10, below.

2. *Ma sendo quelli retti da cagione superiori* — I have attempted

to preserve Machiavelli's use of the singular "cause" (*cagione*) together with an adjective (*superiori*) in the plural. Machiavelli is saying that ecclesiastical principates are upheld by a superior cause — or is it by superior causes? He wishes, it would seem, to have it both ways. I interpret his grammatical error as a desire to indicate that the one Cause of the Biblical tradition is in a certain respect to be equated with the many divine causes of the gentile tradition — that is, with the many gods of the pagans. Thus the superiority of either a Cause or the causes is equally inaccessible to the human mind.

3. Charles VIII entered Italy in 1494. See Ch. III, n. 5, above.

4. It was especially the policy of Lorenzo the Magnificent (1449-1492) to maintain a balance between these powers.

5. On the use of the word "state," see Ch. I, n.3, above.

6. Sixtus IV (1414-1484), born Francesco della Rovere, was pope from 1471 to 1484. He initiated the policy of bringing the northern Papal States more directly under the Pope's control. His name was connected with the Pazzi conspiracy of 1484 against the Medici. The hanging of the Archbishop Salviati by the Florentines as a co-conspirator led to the Pope's excommunication of Lorenzo, the laying of an interdict on Florence, and a war (1478-79). *Florentine Histories,* VIII.1-9.

7. That is, the Orsini could not move quickly enough to extirpate the Colonnas when a pope favorable to the Colonnas was elected.

8. Note that Cesare is only an "instrument" of his father. See Ch. XXVI, n. 2, below. See also *Discourses,* III.29.

9. A tax of one-tenth was imposed on all Christendom by a papal bull of 1500, ostensibly for the crusades against the Turks. Alexander had also made the cardinals pay for their offices and he claimed the right to confiscate the wealth of those cardinals who died. Machiavelli seems to be referring, however, to the sale of indulgences and ecclesiastical offices.

10. On Julius II and his enterprises, see Ch. XXV, nn. 4 and 5 below.

XII

HOW MANY KINDS OF MILITIA[1] THERE ARE AND ABOUT MERCENARY SOLDIERS*

Having discussed in particular all the qualities of those principates which in the beginning I proposed to reason[2] upon, and having considered, in some part, the causes of their well- and ill-being, and having shown the modes with which many have sought to acquire and to keep them, it now remains for me to discuss generally the offenses and defenses which can be adopted by each of those named above. We have said above how necessary it is that a prince have good foundations; otherwise he comes to ruin of necessity. The principal foundations which all states have, whether new, old, or mixed, are good laws and good arms. And because there cannot be good laws where there are not good arms, and where there are good arms there needs must be good laws, I shall omit the reasoning on laws and speak of arms.

I say, then, that the arms with which a prince defends his state are either his own, mercenary, auxiliary, or mixed. Mercenary and auxiliary [arms] are useless and dangerous; and if one keeps his state founded on mercenary arms, he will never be at rest or secure, because those arms are disunited, ambitious, without discipline, unfaithful; valorous among friends, cowardly among

*Quot Sint Genera Militiae et de Mercenariis Militibus

enemies, they do not fear God, nor do they keep faith with men;[3] ruin is delayed only as long as the attack is delayed; such that one is despoiled by them in peace, by enemies in war. The cause of this is that they have no love nor any cause to keep them in the field, other than that of a bit of a stipend, which is not sufficient to make them want to die for you.[4] They are very willing to be your soldiers while you do not make war; but, when war comes, they flee or go away.

I should not have to work very hard to persuade anyone of this point, for the ruin of Italy today is caused by nothing other than her reliance for many years upon mercenary arms. These arms certainly did some service for a few, and they may have seemed valorous when among themselves, but, when the foreigner came, they showed what they were; hence Charles, King of France, was allowed to take Italy with chalk.[5] And he who said that our sins were the cause of this, said the truth;[6] but they were certainly not those which he believed, but those which I have narrated; and because these were sins of princes, they have also suffered the penalty.

I wish to demonstrate better the infelicity of these arms. Mercenary captains[7] are either men excellent in arms or they are not. If they are, then you cannot trust them, because they will always aspire to their own greatness, by either oppressing you, their patron, or by oppressing others quite contrary to your intentions; but if the captain is not virtuous, you are ordinarily ruined. And if one responds that this will happen with anyone who has arms in hand, mercenary or not, I would reply that as arms are employed either by a prince or by a republic that a prince ought in person to take the office of captain; a republic has to send its citizens — and when it sends one who does not prove a worthy man, it ought to replace him, and when he is worthy, keep him within the laws so that he does not overstep the mark. And by experience one sees that single princes and armed republics make very great progress, and that mercenary arms do nothing but damage; and a republic armed with its own arms is with more difficulty brought to obey one of its citizens than one which is armed with foreign arms.

Rome and Sparta were for many centuries armed and free. The Swiss are armed to the highest degree and free to the highest. The Carthaginians are an example of ancient mercenary arms, and they were oppressed by their mercenary soldiers when the first war with the Romans ended, even though the Carthaginians had their own citizens as leaders. After the death of Epaminondas, Philip of Macedon[8] was made captain of their people by the Thebans, and, after he won victory, he took away their liberty. The Milanese hired Francesco Sforza against the Venetians after the Duke Filippo died. After overcoming their enemies at Caravaggio, he joined with them in order to oppress his patrons, the Milanese.[9] Sforza, his father,[10] having been hired by Queen Giovanna of Naples, then left her in one stroke disarmed; whereupon to save the kingdom, she was constrained to throw herself into the lap of the King of Aragon.

And if the Venetians and Florentines have in the past increased their imperium with these arms, yet their captains have not then made themselves princes but have indeed defended them, I respond that the Florentines in this case have been favorites of chance. For of the captains who were virtuous, and therefore to be feared, some won no victories, some had opposition, others turned their ambition elsewhere. The one who did not win [any victories] was Giovanni Acuto [John Hawkwood],[11] and because he never won any battles, the Florentines could not know his faith; but everyone will confess that, had he won, the Florentines would have been at his discretion. The Sforza always had the Bracceschi as their adversaries, so that each watched the other.[12] Francesco turned all his ambition against Lombardy; Braccio against the Church and the Kingdom of Naples. But let us come to that which recently occurred. The Florentines made Paulo Vitelli,[13] a most prudent man, their captain; he had, from private fortune, attained to a very great reputation. Had that man conquered Pisa, no one could deny that it would have been needful for the Florentines to stay with him; for, if he had gone over to soldier for their enemies, they would have had no remedy; and if they had kept him, they would have had to obey him.

And if one considers the progress of the Venetians, one sees that they acted securely and gloriously as long as they made war themselves (this was before they engaged in enterprises on land). With their own gentry and armed plebs they acted very virtuously, but when they began to fight on land, they lost their virtue and followed Italian customs in wars. In the beginning of their augmentation on land, because they had little state[14] there and had a great reputation, they had little to fear from their captains; but as they grew, as they did under Carmignuola,[15] they had a sample of this error, for they saw that he was most virtuous;[16] they had fought the Duke of Milan under his command, and on the other hand, knowing how he had grown cold toward the war, they judged that because he no longer wished to conquer, that they could no longer conquer with him [in command], and yet they could not let him go without losing what they had acquired — thus they were necessitated, in order to secure themselves, to kill him. They then had as their captains Bartolommeo da Bergamo, Roberto da San Severino, the Count of Pitigliano, and the like; with them they had to fear defeat, not their [captains'] gain; as it indeed came to pass at Vailà, where in one battle they lost what, with so much toil, they had acquired in eight hundred years.[17] For from these arms there comes only slow, late, and weak acquisitions, and sudden and miraculous losses. And because I have come with my examples to Italy, which has been for many years governed by mercenary arms, I want to discuss them more from on high, so that having seen the origins and progress of them, one can better correct them.

You[18] have then to understand that, in these recent times, as soon as Italy began to rebel against the Empire, and the Pope gained much reputation in temporal matters, Italy was divided into more states. For many of the great cities took up arms against their nobles, who, as favorites of the Emperor, had formerly oppressed them; and the Church favored the cities so she could gain for herself reputation in temporal matters; and in many of the other [cities], their own citizens became princes.[19] Whereupon Italy came almost completely into the hands of the Church and a few republics; and these priests and other citizens having no knowledge in the use of arms, they began to hire foreigners. The first who gave reputation to this kind of militia was Alberigo da Conio, a Romagnol.[20] From his school there descended, among others, Braccio and Sforza who, in their time, were the arbiters of Italy. After them came all the others who, until our times, have governed these arms. And the result of their virtue has been that Italy has been overrun by Charles, plundered by Louis, violated by Ferdinand and insulted by the Swiss.[21]

The order which they[22] have kept has been, first, to take away the reputation of the infantry to gain reputation for themselves. They did this, because being men without state and [dependent] on their own industry, they were unable to feed many, and a few infantry could not give them reputation. They were therefore reduced to horse, and with a supportable number of these they could feed themselves and gain honors. They were therefore reduced to such terms, that in an army of twenty thousand soldiers, one could not find two thousand infantry. Besides this, they used all their industry to free themselves and their soldiers from toil and fear; they did not kill themselves in skirmishes, but took each other prisoners without ransom. They did not attack towns at night, nor did the towns attack the tents; they constructed neither stockades nor trenches around their camps; they did not campaign in winter. And all these things were permitted by their military orders, which were founded by them to avoid, as has been said, toil and dangers: such that they have conducted[23] Italy into slavery and contempt.

Notes

1. Militia — may mean military service or warfare, or it may refer to military things in general. Thus the different kinds of militia may refer to the different modes of ordering one of man's important activities — warfare — or, to the different modes of ordering the military things.

2. See Ch. II, n. 1, above.

3. On the connection between arms and faith, see *The Art of War,* Bk. 7, and *Discourses,* I.11.

4. The second person familiar is used. See Ch. VI, n.1, above.

5. An expression attributed by the French historian, Philippe de Commines, to Alexander VI. The French, according to the Pope, needed only chalk and wooden spurs to conquer Italy — chalk to mark their lodgings and wooden spurs to prick their mules forward. *Memoirs,* trans. by Andrew R. Scobie (London: Henry G. Bohn, 1865) II, Ch. XIV.

6. This was Savonarola who preached on Nov. 1, 1494 (All Saints' Day) that Charles VIII's entrance into Italy was a scourge of God to the Italians in general and to the Florentines in particular. *Discourses* I.11, 45, 56; III.30. On the true sins, see II.18. See Ch. VI, n.6, above.

7. On the meaning of "captain," see Ch. VIII, n. 4, above.

8. Philip II (382-336 B.C.), the father of Alexander the Great. See Ch. XIII, nn. 13 and 14, below.

9. Francesco Sforza laid claim to the Duchy of Milan in 1447 on the basis of his marriage to Bianca, the illegitimate daughter of Filippo Maria Visconti. His victory at Caravaggio over the Venetians took place in 1448; he then concluded a separate treaty with Venice, besieged Milan in 1449, and forced the city's surrender by famine in March, 1450. *Florentine Histories,* VI. 18-21.

10. Giacomuzzo Attendolo Sforza (1369-1424) took the side of

Louis, the Angevin claimant to the throne of Naples, in 1420. Queen Giovanna II, being without an heir, vacillated between naming Louis II of Anjou or Alfonso of Aragon as her heir. Louis died, but Giovanna adopted his brother, René of Provence, as her heir. Upon her death in 1435, however, Alfonso expelled the Angevins, and established the Aragonese house in Naples. "Sforza" or "the forcer" was a nickname given to Giacomuzzo Attendolo by Alberigo da Barbiano. *Florentine Histories,* I.38.

11. An Englishman in the service of Florence from 1377 to his death in 1393, Hawkwood began his career in Italy as captain-general of a band of English mercenaries known as the White Company. Hawkwood's tactics were characterized by mobility and the use of the long-bow.

12. Bracceschi — The Bracceschi were the followers of Niccolò Fortebraccio, who was also known as Braccio da Montone. Two schools or two orders of military discipline, the Bracceschi and the Sforzeschi, were dominant among the *condottieri* of this period. Both founders had been pupils of Alberigo da Barbiano (see n. 20, below). Braccio took the side of Queen Giovanna and Alfonso of Aragon against Sforza, and from then on the two *condottieri* always opposed each other.

Of the rivalry between the two schools, Machiavelli says:

> Now there were two sects [*sette*] of arms in Italy, Braccesca and Sforzesca: of the latter, the Count Francesco, the son of Sforza, was head; of the other, the principal men were Niccolò Piccino and Niccolò Fortebraccio: nearly all the arms of Italy joined themselves to these sects. Of these, the Sforzesca were in greater esteem, because the Duke of Milan had given him the promise of Madonna Bianca, [the Duke's] natural daughter; the hope of which relation brought him [Francesco] the greatest reputation *(Florentine Histories,* V.2).

The term "sects" is chosen with care. On Machiavelli's use of the term, see Harvey C. Mansfield, Jr., "Party and Sect in Machiavelli's *Florentine Histories,"* in *Machiavelli and the Nature of Political Thought,* ed. by Martin Fleisher (New York: Atheneum, 1972), pp. 209-266. One may note that Machiavelli uses the term when he speaks of the Christians and Muslims. See also *Discourses* II. Preface and 5.

13. For Paulo Vitelli see Ch. VIII, n. 6, above.

14. On the use of the word "state," see Ch. I, n. 3, above.

15. Francesco Bussone, Count of Carmignuola, was executed in May, 1432, for treason, which the Venetian State believed was the only reasonable explanation for his coldness toward the war against Milan. His coldness was such that in the spring of 1432 he refused to accept the proffered surrender of a town and a castle. On the Venetians' suspicion of their mercenaries, see the *Florentine Histories,* VI.3.

16. On the use of the word "virtue," see Ch. I, n. 9, above.

17. The battle of Vailà, also known as the battle of Agnadello (1509), was the first of the serious battles which Italy was to suffer from then on. See Ch. III, n. 5, above. The chivalrous wars of the *condottieri* came to an end. Venice, as a result of the battle, lost all her mainland possessions. See *Discourses,* I.53; III.31.

Bartolommeo Colleoni da Bergamo (1400-1475), whose bronze mounted statue by Verrocchio now standing in the square of San Giovanni e Paulo in Venice makes him a symbol for all the *condottieri,* was a disciple of Sforza, and, after the usual shifts of loyalty, became Captain-General of Venice.

Roberto da San Severino was in the service of Venice during the war against Ferrara in 1482-84.

Niccolò Orsini (1442-1510), Count of Pitigliano, was in service to Venice in 1508-09. He and Bartolommeo d'Alviani commanded the Venetian forces at Vailà. Pitigliano took no part in the battle, since he was still on the march during the engagement. He was known for his caution and slowness in acting.

18. *avete* — The courteous second person is used. See Ch. III, n. 19, above.

19. The names Guelf ("Welf") and Ghibbeline ("Waiblingen") were attached to the papal and imperial parties, respectively, during the struggle for the control of Italy. According to Daniel Waley (*The Italian City-Republics,* World University Library [N.Y. and Toronto: McGraw-Hill, 1969], pp. 200 ff.), the terms came into use in the reign of Frederick II (1220-1250), but became attached to the anti- and pro-imperial parties only in 1265 when the Guelf party became identified with the claims of the House of Anjou. "Welf" was the family name of Otto IV, the Saxon opponent of Frederick II. "Waiblingen" was the name of a Hohenstaufen castle which was used as a battle-cry. It should be noted that the names Guelf and Ghibelline continued in use long after the original conflict which had brought them into being had disappeared. Originally, the party of the merchants and the people were the Guelfs, that of the feudal nobility were the Ghibellines. But in Florence, at the end of the 14th century, the Guelfs had become the oligarchical party. Thus in 1378 there occurred the plebeian uprising of the Ciompi against the Guelfs. See Ch. IX, n. 6, above.

20. Alberigo (or Alberico) da Barbiano, Count of Conio, founded the Company of St. George, the first Italian company of mercenary soldiers. It was he who reintroduced the mounted soldier or the man-at-arms and the tactics suitable for such forces. That is to say, he founded the military modes and orders followed by Braccio, Sforza, and others. He died in 1409.

Machiavelli describes the situation in Italy into which Alberigo came as follows:

> There were in Italy, in these times, many soldiers, English, German and Breton, led partly by those princes who at various times came into Italy, and who partly were sent by the pontiffs when they were in Avignon. With these all the Italian princes waged for some time their wars until finally there arose Lodovico da Conio, a Romagnol, who formed a company of Italian soldiers named after St. George; their virtue and their discipline took away the reputation of foreign arms

in a short time, and gave it back to the Italian, of whom, then, the princes of Italy, in their wars between themselves, availed themselves . . . (*Florentine Histories,* I.34).

21. Overrun by Charles VIII; plundered by Louis XII; violated by Ferdinand the Catholic of Spain; and insulted by the Swiss, who, with their infantry, defeated the Italian mercenaries at Novara in 1500, when Ludovico Sforza was driven out of Milan a second time (Ch. III), and again at Ravenna, in 1512, when, to the surprise of everyone (Ch. XIII), the Swiss turned against the French and thus saved Pope Julius II and the Holy League (which united the Pope, Venice and Spain against France).

22. they — That is, the mercenaries.

23. *condotta* — Machiavelli puns with this word, using it in an unusual way to mean "led." The *condotta* is the contract with a *condottiere,* whose modes of procedure have conducted (*condotta*) Italy into slavery. Cf. *Chief Works,* I, p. 51, n. 4. See Ch. XXV, below, where Pope Julius becomes a "conductor," that is, a *condottiere.* See also Ch. VII, n. 13, above, and the Introduction.

XIII

OF SOLDIERS: AUXILIARIES, MIXED AND ONE'S OWN*

Auxiliary arms, which are the other useless arms, are those of a power who is called to come to aid and defend you[1] with his arms: as was done in recent times by Pope Julius, who, having seen the sad test of his mercenary arms in the enterprise of Ferrara, turned toward auxiliaries and agreed with Ferdinand, King of Spain, that he should aid him with his people and armies. These arms can be useful and good in themselves, but they are almost always harmful for the one who calls them in, because if they lose, you are left undone; if they win, you are left their prisoner.

And although ancient histories are full of such examples, I nevertheless do not wish to omit this fresh example of Pope Julius II, whose part could not have been less considered, for in wanting Ferrara, he thrust all into the hands of a foreigner. But his good fortune gave rise to a third circumstance,[2] so that he did not gather the fruit of his bad choice; for when his auxiliaries were beaten at Ravenna, the Swiss rose up, outside of every expectation, his as well as the others, and chased out the victors; and it came about that he neither remained a prisoner of his enemies, who had fled, nor of his auxiliaries, for he had won with arms other than

*De Militibus Auxiliariis, Mixtis et Propriis.

theirs.[3] The Florentines, being wholly unarmed, brought in ten thousand Frenchmen to conquer Pisa; by which decision they brought more danger to themselves than at any other time of their troubles.[4] The Emperor of Constantinople, in order to oppose himself to his neighbors, put ten thousand Turks in Greece who, when the war ended, did not want to leave. It was the beginning of the servitude of Greece under the infidels.[5]

Let him, then, who wishes not to win, avail himself of these arms, for they are much more dangerous than mercenary ones. With them one's ruin is made: they are wholly united, are wholly under the obedience of others; but mercenaries need more time and better occasion to harm you, though they may have won, for they do not form a single body, having been found and paid by you. Therefore a third person whom you have made their head cannot immediately gain enough authority to harm you. In sum, in mercenaries indolence is most dangerous; in auxiliaries, virtue.

A wise prince, therefore, has always avoided these arms and turned to his own. He has wished rather to lose with his own than to win with those of others, judging that it is not a true victory which with alien arms has been acquired. I shall never doubt of citing Cesare Borgia and his actions. This Duke entered the Romagna with auxiliary arms, conducting only French troops, and with them he took Imola and Forlì. But when such arms no longer appeared to him safe, he turned to mercenaries, judging that these were less dangerous, and he hired the Orsini and Vitelli. Finding them uncertain and unfaithful and dangerous to manage, he then extinguished them,[6] and turned to his own. One can easily see the difference between the one and the other of these arms, if one considers the difference in the reputation of the Duke when he first had only the French, then when he had the Orsini and Vitelli, and finally, when he was left with his own soldiers and himself to depend on; and one will find it always growing — never was he so esteemed than when everyone saw that he was entirely the possessor of his own arms.

I did not want to depart from Italian and fresh examples, yet I do not want to omit Hiero of Syracuse, who was one of those named above by me.[7] That man, as I said, was made the head of the armies by the Syracusans. He immediately came to know that that mercenary militia was not useful, because it was like our Italian *condottieri;* and since it seemed to him that he could neither keep them nor let them go, he had them all cut into pieces: and from then on he waged war with his own arms and not alien ones. I wish also to recall to memory a figure of the Old Testament, made for this point. When David offered himself to Saul to fight Goliath the Philistine challenger, Saul, in order to give him courage, armed him with his own arms, which, as soon as David had them on, he rejected, saying that he could not be of as good worth with them as by himself, and that he therefore wished to find the enemy with his sling and with his knife.[8] In fine, the arms of others either fall off your back, weigh you down, or constrict you.

Charles VII, father of King Louis XI, having liberated France from the English with his fortune and virtue, knew this necessity of arming oneself with one's own arms, and he established in his kingdom an ordinance for men-at-arms and infantry.[9] Afterwards his son, King Louis, extinguished that ordinance concerning the infantry and began to hire Swiss,[10] and that error, followed by others is the cause, as we in fact now see, of the dangers of that kingdom. For, having given reputation to the Swiss, he debased all his arms; the infantry was wholly extinguished and he made his men-at-arms dependent on the arms of others. Having become accustomed to soldiering with the Swiss, they came to suppose that they could not win without them: from whence it arises that the French are not enough against the Swiss, and, without the Swiss, they refuse to test themselves against others. The armies of France, then, are mixed: in part mercenary and in part their own. These arms are, as a whole, much better than those which are simply auxiliary or simply mercenary, but much inferior to those which are one's own. It is sufficient to have mentioned this example; for the kingdom of France would have been unconquerable had the ordinance of Charles been either augmented or preserved. But the little prudence of men leads them to begin something solely to know present good, and it is not aware of the underlying poison: as I have said above of consumptive fevers.[11]

Therefore he who does not recognize evils when they are being born in a principate, is not truly wise; and this is given to few. And if one considers the first cause of the ruin of the Roman Empire, one will discover that it began only with the hiring of the Goths. From that beginning the weakening of the forces of the Roman Empire commenced, and all that virtue which was in the Romans was given to them. I conclude then, that without having its own arms, no principate is secure; on the contrary, it is wholly obligated to fortune, not having that virtue which with faith defends it in adversity. It has always been the opinion and the saying of wise men, "That nothing is so infirm and unstable as the fame of power which does not rest upon one's own strength."[12] One's own arms are those which are composed either of subjects or of citizens or your own dependents; all others are either mercenaries or auxiliaries. And the mode of ordering one's own arms will be easy to find, if one will discuss the orders of the four named above by me,[13] if one will see how Philip, father of Alexander the Great,[14] and how many republics and princes have armed and ordered themselves: to which orders, I, in all things, consign myself.[15]

Notes

1. The second person familiar is used. See Ch. VI, n. 1, above.

2. Julius II hurled himself impetuously into a war with Bologna and Ferrara in September, 1510. The French moved against him in the spring of 1511, touching off a rebellion in Bologna (May 21) which forced the papal armies to flee (the first circumstance). The Pope then formed an alliance with Venice and Spain (the

Holy League) in October, 1511 (the second circumstance). The armies of the French and the League met in battle at Ravenna (April 11, 1512), where the intervention of the Swiss on behalf of the Pope was decisive (the third circumstance). For the references to Julius II in the *Discourses*, see Ch. XXV, n. 5, below.

3. The battle of Ravenna is described as one "more terrible than any other in the memory of man: it was in short the first great battle of modern times . . ." Pasquale Villari, *The Life and Times of Machiavelli* (London: T. Fisher Unwin, first published 1878), II, p. 4. The French won a great victory, but lost their brilliant young commander, Gaston de Foix, and then, as Machiavelli says, the whole world came against them: the Swiss, the Emperor, and England allied themselves with the Holy League. The French were driven out of Italy after the battle of Novara in 1513. *Discourses*, II.16, 17; III.10 end.

4. See the *Discourses*, III.43; and the *First Decennale*. According to the *First Decennale*, Florence's time of troubles begin in 1494 with Charles VIII's invasion of Italy.

5. John Cantacuzene (1291-1380), in his struggle against the Paleologue dynasty, hired ten thousand Turkish horse, with Soliman, the son of the Sultan, at their head. In so doing, he gave the Turks their first foothold in Europe. Overwhelmed by troubles, he retired in 1355 to a monastery where he devoted himself to writing histories. See Gibbon, *Decline and Fall of the Roman Empire*, III, Ch. LXIV.

6. See Ch. VII, above. The *capi* or chieftains of the Orsini and the Vitelli were extinguished at Sinigaglia.

7. See Ch. VI, above.

8. I Samuel, 17:38-40, 45-47. *Discourses*, I.19, 26.

To have one's own arms is to make and to use arms according to the modes and orders proper and fitting to one's own nature and "humor" (See Ch. XXV). A young man accustomed to light arms ought not use the arms of an older man; a cautious man ought not use the arms of an impetuous and bold man; nor should a compassionate man order his arms as would one with a harsh and bitter nature. See *Discourses,* III.21.

9. Charles VII (1403-1461) did for France what Machiavelli hopes will be done by someone for Italy. During the Hundred Years War "free companies" of professional men-at-arms, grouped, in *routes* and therefore also known as *routiers,* were formed, from whom the *condottieri* of Italy were directly descended. To replace these free companies, an ordinance established "companies of the king," each consisting of "100 lances," each lance being one man-at-arms with five more lightly armed attendants. In 1446, "the companies of petty ordinance" were established which were less well-armed. In 1448, a body of infantry was organized; every community had to provide one "free archer" ("free" because they were exempted from taxation) for every fifty hearths. This was a civic militia. The men armed themselves and practised archery once a week.

10. Louis XI (1423-1483) reorganized the French armies in 1474. He disbanded the free archers for their cowardice and lack of discipline, and replaced them with bought infantry of Swiss and Germans. The reign of Louis XI usually marks the close of the feudal order and the beginning of the modern monarchy.

11. See Ch. III, above.

12. *Quod nihil sit tam infirmum aut instabile quam fama potentiae non sua vi nixa,* Tacitus, *Annals* XIII.19. The passage in Tacitus is: *nihil rerum mortalium tam instabile ac fluxum est quam fama potentiae non sua vi nixa* — "Nothing of mortal things is so unstable and uncertain as the fame of power that does not rest upon one's own strength."

13. Machiavelli may not only be referring to the four mentioned in this chapter (Cesare, Hiero of Syracuse, David and Charles VII), but also to the four mentioned in Chapter VI (Moses, Cyrus, Romulus and Theseus). Hiero of Syracuse is added to the list of

Chapter VI, and Philip of Macedon to the list here in Chapter XIII. We have thus two lists, each naming five men, in whose modes and orders Machiavelli reposes his faith.

14. On Philip of Macedon, father of Alexander the Great, see *Discourses*, I.9, 20, 26, 31, 59; II.13, 28; III.6.

15. *a quali ordini io al tutto mi rimetto* — the meaning of *rimettersi* is "to deliver oneself over, to consign oneself to someone or something"; that is, to rely entirely upon someone or something. In Chapter XXIII, the last paragraph, below, Machiavelli speaks of an unwise prince who by chance consigns himself entirely to a prudent counselor, and he there also uses *rimettersi* — *si gia a sorte non si rimettessi in uno solo che al tutto lo governassi* ("unless by chance he consigns himself to one who alone will wholly govern him"). One may also speak of resigning oneself, that is, yielding oneself to another — as when one says that he resigns himself to God's will. Thus it would seem that as an unwise prince should give himself over completely to a prudent counselor, so Machiavelli gives himself over completely to these orders. Here at the center of the work, he thus confesses his faith. See also Ch. VIII, n. 9, above.

XIV

WHAT A PRINCE SHOULD DO
ABOUT THE MILITIA*[1]

A prince, then, ought to have no other object nor any other thought, nor take anything else for his art, but war, its orders and its discipline; for this is the only art awaiting one who commands. And it is of such virtue, that not only does it maintain those who are born princes, but many times men of private fortune rise to that degree by it; and one sees, on the contrary, that princes, when they have thought more of the niceties of life than of arms, have lost their state. And the first cause that makes you[2] lose it is to neglect this art; and the cause that makes you acquire it is to be professed in this art.

Francesco Sforza by being armed, from a private [man] became Duke of Milan; and his sons, by avoiding the hardships of arms, from dukes became private [men]. For among the other consequences[3] which the evil of being disarmed brings upon you, you are made contemptible; and this is one of those infamies from which the prince ought to guard himself, as will be said below. For between someone who is armed and someone who is unarmed, there is no proportion whatsoever; and it is not reasonable that he who is armed willingly obeys him who is unarmed, nor that the unarmed be secure among armed servants. Since there is disdain

*Quod Principem Deceat Circa Militiam.

on the one side, and suspicion on the other, it is impossible that they work well together. Therefore, among other infelicities which have been mentioned, a prince who does not himself understand military things cannot be esteemed by his soldiers, nor can he have trust in them.

He ought, therefore, never to lift his thought from the exercise of war, and he ought to exercise more in peace than in war, which he can do in two modes: one with works, and the other with the intellect.[4] And, as for works, besides keeping his own arms well-ordered and exercised, he ought to be always out on the chase, and by that means to accustom his body to hardships and also in part to learn the nature of sites — to know how the mountains rise, how valleys open, how the plains lie, and to understand the nature of rivers and marshes — and in this to put the greatest of care. This knowledge is useful in two modes: first, he learns to know his own country, and he can better understand how to defend it; and then, by means of his knowledge and experience of these sites, he will comprehend easily any other site that he may necessarily have to examine for the first time. For the hillocks, valleys, rivers and marshes in, for example, Tuscany, have a certain similitude to those in other provinces; so that from the knowledge of a site in one province one can easily come to a knowledge of the others.[5] And that prince who lacks this ability lacks the first requirement of a captain;[6] for this teaches one how to find the enemy, choose encampments, lead armies, prepare the order of battle, and lay siege to towns to your advantage.

Among the praises that have been given by writers to Philopoemen,[7] prince of the Achaeans, it is said that in times of peace he never thought of anything but the modes of war. And when he was in the countryside with his friends, he often stopped and reasoned with them: "If the enemy were on that hill, and we were to be found here with our army, which of us would have the advantage? How would we advance to find them and still keep our order? If we should want to retreat, how should we do it? If they were to retreat, how should we follow them?" And, as he went along, he put to them all the chances which may befall an army. He listened to their opinions, expressed his own and corroborated it with reasons; such that, because of these continued cogitations, whenever he led the armies there could arise no accident for which he did not have the remedy.

But as for the exercise of the intellect, the prince ought to read histories, and to consider in them the actions of excellent men: to see how they governed themselves in wars, to examine the causes of their victories and losses, in order to avoid the latter and to imitate the former; and, above all, to do as has been done in the past by some excellent man, who has chosen to imitate someone before him who was praised and glorified, and who always kept his deeds and actions before him, as it is said that Alexander the Great imitated Achilles; Caesar, Alexander; Scipio, Cyrus. And whoever reads the life of Cyrus written by Xenophon,[8] will immediately recognize in the life of Scipio[9] how much, in chastity, affability, humanity and liberality, Scipio conformed himself to the things of Cyrus that Xenophon has written.[10] A wise prince ought to observe these same modes and never be lazy in peaceful times, but with industry make capital of them, in order to have their value in adversities, so that when fortune changes, he will be found ready to resist them.[11]

Notes

1. The subject is the art of warfare and how the prince must become professed in it to the exclusion of everything else. This subject is the highest one: the proper preparation of the body and the intellect of the prince, the highest kind of man. The term "militia" is therefore used here in the most general sense of either the military things or the things of war. See Ch. XII, n.1, above. See also Ch. XVII, n.15, below.

2. The second person familiar is used. See Ch.VI, n.1, above.

3. *cagioni* — Machiavelli uses *cagioni* or "causes" here.

4. *Opere, mente* — translated here respectively as "works," and "intellect."

5. See also *Discourses* III.39 — "That a captain ought to be a knower of sites." Compare with the Epistle Dedicatory, above, where a prince is said to know the low places but not the high ones. Here it is said that a prince should know all the sites.

6. See Ch. VIII, n. 4, above.

7. Philopoemen of Megalopolis (253-182 B.C.) was the ablest general of the Achaean League, and instituted reforms in the arms and order of battle of the Achaeans. Plutarch, in his *Lives,* speaks of how he transformed the Achaean love of luxury into a love for arms:

> . . . For being long used to vie with each other in their dress, and furniture of the houses, and service of their tables, and to glory in outdoing one another, the disease by custom was grown incurable, and there was no possibility of removing it altogether. But he diverted the passion, and brought them, instead of these superfluities, to love useful and more manly display, and reducing their other expenses, to take delight in appearing magnificent in their equipage of war . . . When Philopoemen had obtained of them to arm, and set themselves out in this manner, he proceeded to train them, mustering and exercising them perpetually; in which they obeyed him with great zeal and eagerness . . . (trans. by John Dryden and revised by Arthur Hugh Clough, Mod. Lib. ed., pp. 440-441.)

It should be remembered, nevertheless, that it was in Philopoemen's time that the Greeks came under Roman rule.

8. See Ch. VI, n. 3, above.

9. Scipio Africanus Major, P. Cornelius (236?-182 B.C.). He was appointed by the People to the command in Spain (210), the first *privatus* to be given pro-consular imperium. *Discourses,* I.10, 11, 29, 53, 58, 60; III.9, 19, 20, 21, 31, 34.

10. On Xenophon (ca. 430?-360? B.C.) see *Discourses*, II.2, 13; III.20, 22, 39. He is the one student of Socrates whom Machiavelli cites in *The Prince*, but his citations are all from the *Cyropaedia*, which is about the education of a barbarian prince. Xenophon was a private man, a general, a historian and a philosopher who presented himself as a wholly practical man. One may therefore perhaps understand Machiavelli's attraction to Xenophon because the latter seems far more concerned than either Plato or Aristotle with the "effectual truth" of things as opposed to the "ineffectual truth." See Ch. XV, n. 1, below.

11. What is to be resisted are the adversities, not fortune. See Ch. XX, below, where the first reference to fortune as a willing and acting being occurs.

XV

OF THOSE THINGS FOR WHICH MEN, AND ESPECIALLY PRINCES, ARE PRAISED OR BLAMED

It remains now to see what the modes and government of a prince ought to be with respect to his subjects and his friends. And because I know that many have written on this, I fear that I shall be taken to be presumptuous in writing about it again, especially in my departing from the orders of others in the disputation of this matter. But since it is my intention to write a useful thing for him who understands, it seemed to me more profitable to go behind to the effectual truth[1] of the thing, than to the imagination thereof. And many have imagined republics and principates that have never been seen or known to be in truth; because there is such a distance between how one lives and how one should live that he who lets go that which is done for that which ought to be done learns his ruin rather than his preservation — for a man who wishes to profess the good in everything needs must fall among so many who are not good. Hence it is necessary for a prince, if he wishes to maintain himself, to learn to be able to be not good, and to use it and not use it according to the necessity.

De His Rebus Quibus Homines et Praesertim Principes Laudantur aut Vituperantur.

Omitting, then, the things about an imagined prince, and discussing those which are true, I say that all men, whenever one speaks of them, and most especially princes, since they are placed so high, are noted for some of these qualities which bring them either blame or praise. And thus it is that some are held liberal, some *misero* (using a Tuscan term, because *avaro* in our language still denotes one who desires to have by rapine; *misero* we call the one who abstains much from using his own); some are held to be givers, others rapacious; some cruel, others full of pity;[2] the one faithless, the other faithful; the one effeminate and pusillanimous, the other fierce and spirited; the one human, the other proud; the one lascivious, the other chaste; the one open, the other cunning; the one hard, the other easy; the one grave, the other light; the one religious, the other skeptical, and the like.[3]

And I know that everyone will confess that it would be a most praiseworthy thing to find in a prince all the qualities written above which are held to be good. But because one is not able to have or observe them wholly, for human conditions do not allow it, it is necessary for him to be so prudent that he will know how to avoid the infamy of those vices which would lose him the state; and, if it is possible, to guard himself against those which will not take it away; but, if he cannot, he can with less concern let them go. And, further, he should not concern himself about incurring the infamy of those vices without which it would be difficult to save the state; for, if one will consider everything well, he will find something which will seem virtue itself, and his conforming to it would be his ruin; and something other which will seem vice itself, and his conforming to it would succeed in security and the good being his.

Notes

1. *la verità effetuale* — The "effectual truth" as distinguished from the "ineffectual truth," signifies that Machiavelli is not in-

terested in truth as such, but in that truth which may be put into practice. We are here, in Chapter XV of *The Prince,* at the beginning of the modern concern with the justification or confirmation of theory by practice. Not contemplation but successful practice is the end of thought.

2. See Ch. XVII, n. 1, below.

3. Cf. Aristotle's discussion of the virtues concerned with the passions in the *Nicomachean Ethics* 1106b33-1108b9.

If *avaro* is included in the list, we have a list of twelve vices and eleven virtues — *avaro* is a vice with no corresponding virtue (or is it neither vice nor virtue?). Otherwise there is a list of eleven corresponding virtues and vices. If the virtues of liberality and giving are not to be distinguished — and Prof. Strauss points out that Machiavelli says in Chapter XVI that they are not to be — and *avaro* is not included, then there is a list of 10. One is left puzzled as to what should or should not be included in the list; it is also an incomplete one, and the list itself shows no discernible order, for he sometimes lists a virtue first, and sometimes a vice. See Strauss, *Thoughts on Machiavelli,* pp. 337-339 (n. 139 of Ch. IV).

XVI

OF LIBERALITY AND PARSIMONY*

Let me begin, then, with the first of the qualities written above. I say that it would be good to be reputed to be liberal. Nevertheless, liberality used in such a mode that gains you[1] reputation for it, harms you; because if it is used virtuously and in the mode one ought to use it,[2] it may not be recognized, and you will not escape the infamy of its opposite. For, if one wishes to maintain the name of liberal among men, it is necessary that one not omit any quality of sumptuousness — to such an extent, that a prince so disposed will consume all his faculties in such-like works, and he will be finally necessitated, in his wish to maintain the name of liberal, to burden the people extraordinarily, to become exacting, and do all those things that can be done to get money. This will begin to make him hateful to his subjects and, as he becomes poor, none of them will respect him; in such a mode that, having harmed the many with this his liberality, and rewarded the few, he will feel every mischance which first arises and he will be endangered by every danger which appears. Coming to know this and wishing to draw back, he then immediately incurs the infamy of stinginess.

De Liberalitate et Parsimonia.

Since a prince, therefore, cannot use this virtue of liberality in such a mode as to become known for it without harm, he ought not, if he is prudent, care about the name of stinginess; for in time he will always be held to be most liberal, since his parsimony will make his income suffice — he can then defend himself from whoever makes war on him; he can undertake enterprises without burdening the people; such that he may be liberal to everyone from whom he takes nothing, and these are infinite in number, and he will be stingy with all those to whom he does not give, and these will be few. In our times we have seen great things done only by those reputed to be stingy; all the others have been extinguished. Pope Julius II, although he served the name of liberality in order to attain to the papacy, never thought afterwards of maintaining that name so that he would be able to make war; the present King of France has waged many wars without levying an extraordinary tax on his own people, and this was possible only because his extra expenses were covered by his long-practised parsimony. The present King of Spain would not have undertaken or won so many enterprises had he been reputed to be liberal.

A prince, therefore, ought little to esteem, in order not to have to rob his subjects, in order to be able to defend himself, in order not to become poor and despised, in order not to be forced to become rapacious, incurring the name of stinginess; because this is one of those vices which enables him to reign. And if someone were to say: Caesar with his liberality obtained the imperium, and many others, by being and by having been held to be liberal, have attained to very great rank — I respond: either you have already become a prince, or you are on the way to acquiring [that rank]: in the first case, this liberality is harmful; in the second, it is very necessary to be reputed liberal. Caesar was one of those who wished to attain to the principate of Rome; but, after he had arrived there, had he survived and not tempered his spending, he would have destroyed that imperium.[3] And if someone were to reply, many have been princes who have been reputed to be extremely liberal, and yet they have done great things with their armies — I respond to you [as follows]: either a prince spends his own and that of his subjects, or he spends that which belongs to others — in the first case, he ought to be frugal; in the other, he ought not to omit any part of liberality.

And for the prince who with his armies lives on plunder, sack and ransom, who handles what belongs to others, it is necessary that he exercise liberality; otherwise, he will not be followed by his soldiers. And of that which does not belong to you or your subjects, you can be a very great giver, as were Cyrus,[4] Caesar and Alexander;[5] for the spending of what belongs to others does not take away your reputation, but adds to it. It is only the spending of what is yours that hurts you. And there is nothing that consumes itself so much as liberality, for you lose the faculty for using it all the while that you use it, and become either poor and despised, or, to avoid poverty, rapacious and hated. And above all other things, a prince ought to guard against being despised and hated, and liberality conducts you to one or the other. Therefore, it is far wiser to have the name of stinginess, which begets an infamy without hatred, rather than to be necessitated, by wanting the name of liberal, to incur the name of rapacious which begets an infamy with hatred.

Notes

1. The second person familiar is used.

2. On proper giving, see Aristotle, *Nicomachean Ethics,* 1119b22-1122a18, and Matthew 6:2-4.

3. On Julius Caesar (100-44 B.C.), see *Discourses,* I.10, 17, 29, 33, 34, 37, 46, 52, 29; III.6, 13, 24. On the usage of the term "imperium," see Ch. I, n. 4, above.

4. See Ch. VI, n. 3, above, for the references in the *Discourses* to Cyrus.

5. See Ch. IV, n. 1, above, for the references in the *Discourses* to Alexander the Great.

XVII

OF CRUELTY AND PITY: AND IF IT IS BETTER TO BE LOVED THAN FEARED, OR THE CONTRARY*

Descending then to the other previously mentioned qualities, I say that every prince ought to desire to be reputed to be full of pity[1] and not held to be cruel; nevertheless, he ought to take heed that he not use this pity badly. Cesare Borgia was held to be cruel; nevertheless, that cruelty of his repaired the Romagna, united it, and reduced it to peace and faith.[2] If one will consider this well, one will see that he had much more pity than the Florentine people, who, in order to avoid the name of cruel, let Pistoia be destroyed.[3] Therefore, a prince ought not to care about the infamy of cruelty with respect to keeping his subjects united and faithful; for, with very few examples [of cruelty], he will be able to show more pity than those who, by too much pity, allow disorders to follow, from which arise murders or rapine; because these usually harm an entire body,[4] while those executions which come from a prince harm someone in particular. And of all princes, it is especially impossible for a new prince to avoid the name of cruelty, because new states are full of dangers. And Virgil, through the mouth of Dido says: "Difficult things and a new reign force me to take such measures, and to defend the boundaries all around."[5]

*De Crudelitate et Pietate; et an Sit Melius Amari Quam Timeri, Vel e Contra.

Nevertheless, he ought to be deliberate in belief and action,[6] nor should he make fear for himself;[7] and he should proceed in such a mode, tempered with prudence and humanity, so that too much confidence not make him incautious and too much diffidence not render him intolerable.[8]

From this arises a dispute: whether it is better to be loved than feared, or the reverse. One may respond that one would wish to be both the one and the other, but since it is difficult to mix these qualities together, it is much safer to be feared than loved, if one of the two must be lacking. For one can say this generally of men: that they are ungrateful, fickle, hypocrites and dissemblers, evaders of dangers, lovers of gain; and while you[9] do them good, they are wholly yours, offering you blood, goods, life, and sons, as has been said above,[10] when need is far off; but when it approaches you, then they revolt. And that prince who founds himself wholly upon their words, if he finds himself naked in other preparations, will be ruined. For friends which one acquires for a price, and not with greatness and nobility of mind — one merits them, but one does not have them — when the time comes they cannot be spent. And men are less cautious about offending one who has made himself loved, than one who has made himself feared; for love is maintained by a chain of obligation which, because of men's wickedness, is broken on every occasion of their own utility; but fear is maintained by a dread of punishment which never abandons you.

The prince, nevertheless, ought to make himself feared in such a mode that if he does not acquire love, he then avoids hatred; for being feared and not hated can go very well together; and he will always bring this about, if he abstains from the goods of his citizens and subjects, and from their women. If it becomes needful to proceed against the blood of someone, he should do so when there is suitable justification and manifest cause; but, above all, he should himself abstain from the goods of others, for men forget more quickly the death of a father than the loss of patrimony. Moreover, causes for taking goods are never lacking, and he who begins to live by rapine will always find cause for taking that which belongs to others; while, on the contrary, causes to proceed against the blood are very rare and are very quickly lacking.

But when the prince is with his armies and has multitudes of soldiers under his government, then is it wholly necessary not to care about the name of cruelty. Without that name, one cannot keep his army united or disposed to any deed. Among the wonderful actions of Hannibal one numbers this: that having a very great army which was a mixture of infinite races of men, which he had conducted to war in alien lands, there never arose any dissension, neither among themselves, nor against the prince, in bad as well as in good fortune. That lack of dissension could not have proceeded from anything other than his inhuman cruelty which, together with his infinite virtues, always made him, in the eyes of his soldiers, venerated and terrible. Without that cruelty his other virtues would not have been sufficient to bring about that effect. And the writers on this point have insufficiently thought about it; on the one hand they admire his action and on the other, they condemn the principal cause of it.[11]

And to see that it is true that his other virtues would not have sufficed, one can consider in Scipio, a most rare man not only of his time, but in the memory of all things that are known. His armies rebelled in Spain, and this did not proceed from anything other than his excessive pity, which permitted his soldiers more license than was fitting for military discipline. This brought him reproof from Fabius Maximus[12] in the Senate, and he was called the corrupter of the Roman militia. And the Locrians, whose city had been sacked by Scipio's legate, were not avenged by him, nor was the insolence of that legate corrected[13] — all of which proceeded from his easy nature: to such an extent that, someone in the Senate who wished to excuse him[14] said that, there were many men who knew better how not to err than how to correct errors. This nature of his would have, in time, wronged Scipio's fame and glory, had he continued with it in the imperium,[15] but since he lived under the government of the Senate, this harmful quality was not only hidden, but brought him to glory.

I conclude then, returning to the question of being feared or loved, that since men love at their own pleasure and fear at the prince's pleasure, a wise prince should found himself on that which is his, not on that which is dependent upon others — he ought only to contrive to avoid hatred, as has been said.

Notes

1. *pietoso* — Machiavelli uses the terms *pietà* and *pietoso*, which are usually translated as "mercy" and "merciful," but these terms are more accurately translated as "piety" and "piteous." "Piety" has the meaning, now obsolete, of "pity" or "mercy," but it also refers to a man's godliness or religious devotion, and a "piteous" man could then be pious or merciful or both. The choice then is between being cruel on the one hand, or being pious *and* full of pity on the other. Cf. Ch. XXI, where Ferdinand of Spain is said to have turned to a *pietosa crudeltà*, a "pious cruelty" or "cruel pity." Cruel pity would seem to be that pity, as the remark on the Florentine people would imply, which led to greater cruelty being done. Cruel pity would then need to be distinguished from "cruelty well-used" (Ch. VIII).

2. *ridottola in pace et in fede* — To reduce, that is, to restore or bring back, but with the implication of compulsion, as when one reduces a town into ruins. As Machiavelli previously has said, his *credo* is in cruelty well-used (Ch. VIII); and in arms making men believe (Ch. VI), as well as making good laws (Ch. XII).

3. Pistoia was divided by factions, and instead of extinguishing them, as Cesare Borgia extinguished the lords of the Romagna, the Florentines permitted the disorders to continue, letting the

factions in the city destroy one another. The consequence was that Pistoia was torn apart by riots, and the city suffered greatly. See Ch. XX, below.

4. *una universalità intera* — What Machiavelli seems to mean is that some entire body or corporation of society will be harmed. See Ch. XIX, n. 7, below.

5. *Res dura et regni novitas me tali cogunt/Moliri, et late fines custode tueri.* — *Aeneid* I, 563-564.

6. *essere grave al credere e al muoversi* — An older translation is: "to be judicious in his giving belief to any thing, or moving himself thereat" (the 1640 trans. by Edward Dacres with an introduction by Henry Cust [London: D. Nutt, 1905], I, 318. Hereafter cited as the Dacres translation). Machiavelli seems to mean that the prince must show himself to be a serious man in his outward conduct.

7. *ne si fare paura da se stesso* — The Dacres translation is, "nor make his people extreamly afraid of him." But the meaning seems to be, not to be easily frightened, that is, not to make oneself afraid by manufacturing or imagining fears.

8. One should perhaps also interpret the confidence and diffidence of the prince as referring not only to his opinion of others, that is, whether or not he excessively trusts or distrusts them, but to his opinion of his own powers. A man who has too low an opinion of his virtues would make himself contemptible in the eyes of the people. Not to know one's own worth leads others to wonder about one's capacities; and to be overly confident of one's powers has its obvious dangers.

9. The second person familiar is used. See Ch. VI, n.1, above.

10. See Ch. IX, above.

11. That is, they admire his capacity to unite an army comprised of "infinite races," but condemn the cruelty which enabled him to

keep it united. On Hannibal (247 - 183 or 182 B.C.), see the *Discourses* II.18.27; III.9, 10, 21, 40. See also n. 15, below.

12. On Quintus Fabius Maximus Cunctator (d. 203 B.C.), see the *Discourses,* I.53; III.9, 19. But Machiavelli treats two Fabii as if they were one, or, more precisely, as if they were alike in kind (*Discourses,* III.46). The other, and earlier, Fabius is Quintus Fabius Maximus Rullianus (d. 290 B.C.) for which see the *Discourses,* I.31; II.33; III.1, 33, 36, 45, 47, 49. Fabius Cunctator was the great opponent of Hannibal in the Second Punic War (219-201); Fabius Rullianus was consul several times during the period of the Samnite Wars (343-290). For the significance of "Fabius," see Strauss, *Thoughts on Machiavelli,* pp. 106-107, 118, 132, 152-153, 157, 165, 166-167, 173, 246. See also n. 15, below.

13. The officer was Quintus Pleminius, *legatus pro praetore* in 205 B.C. He looted Locri, not sparing the treasury of Persephone. Scipio kept him in command and the Senate had to intervene, arresting and imprisoning Quintus Pleminius.

14. One of the ambassadors from Locri.

15. *nello imperio* — could also mean "into the empire." That is, one could read this passage as: "which nature of his would have in time wronged Scipio's fame and glory, had he continued into the Empire with it" (see Musa's translation). But imperium, that is, the supreme command, seems the more likely meaning. See Ch. I, n. 4, above, and the Introduction.

The final judgment on Scipio cannot be made until after careful consideration of the discussion of cruelty and pity in the *Discourses,* III. 19-22. The comparison between Hannibal and Scipio, between a cruel nature and an easy one, is to be found in III.21.

Hannibal, Fabius and Scipio seem to represent the three most important kinds of men. Chapter XIV, one may say, treats of the formation of the prince, while Chapter XVII treats of the matter or the body (that is, the nature) of the prince who is to be formed. See also Ch. IV, n. 11, above, and Ch. XXV, below.

XVIII

IN WHAT MODE PRINCES OUGHT TO
KEEP FAITH*

How praiseworthy it is for a prince to maintain faith and to live by integrity and not by cunning, everyone understands; nevertheless one sees by experience, in our times, that those princes who have done great things have taken little account of faith, and have also known with cunning how to go round the brains of men; and in the end they have surpassed those who have founded themselves on loyalty.

You[1] ought to know, then, that there are two kinds of fighting: one with the laws, the other with force. The first one is proper to man; the second to the beasts; but because the first proves many times to be insufficient, one needs must resort to the second. Therefore it is necessary for a prince to know well how to use the beast and the man. This part has been covertly taught to princes by the ancient writers, who wrote that Achilles and many other ancient princes were given to the care of Chiron the centaur, so that he might look after them under his discipline.[2] To say this is simply to wish to say that one has to have as a preceptor one who is half-beast and half-man, that it is needful for a prince to know how to use the one and the other nature, and that the one without the other is not durable.

Quomodo Fides a Principibus Sit Servanda.

Since a prince must of necessity know well how to use the beast, he ought of the beasts to pick the fox and the lion;[3] for the lion cannot defend himself from snares, and the fox cannot defend himself from wolves. One needs, then, to be fox to know snares, and lion to terrify wolves. Those who rely simply on the lion do not understand this. A prudent lord, therefore, cannot, nor ought he, observe faith, when such observance turns against him and the causes which made him give his promise are extinguished. And if all men were good, this precept would not be good; but since they are wicked, and would not be faithful to you,[4] you also do not have to be faithful to them. Nor does a prince ever lack legitimate causes to color his inobservance. Of this one could give infinite modern examples and show how many peace treaties and how many promises have been of no effect and made vain by the infidelity of princes — and those who have known best how to use the fox, have turned out best. But it is necessary to this nature to know how to color it, and to be a great hypocrite and deceiver, and men are so simple, and so obedient to present necessity, that he who deceives will always find one who will let himself be deceived.

I do not wish to be silent about one of these recent examples. Alexander VI never did anything else and he never thought about anything else but how to deceive men, and he always found a subject for his practice. And there never was a man who was more efficacious in asseverating, or with greater oaths affirmed a thing, who less observed [his faith]. Nevertheless, his deceptions always succeeded at his will, because he knew so well this part of the world.

It is not necessary, then, for a prince to have in fact all of the qualities written above, but it is indeed necessary to appear to have them. I shall rather dare to say this: that having them and observing them always, they are harmful, but in appearing to have them, they are useful — so as to appear to be full of pity, faithful, human, open, religious, and to be so, but with one's mind constructed in such a mode that when the need not to be arises, you can, and know how to, change to the contrary. And this has to be understood, that a prince, and especially a new prince, cannot observe all those things by which men are held to be good, for they are often necessitated to work against faith, against charity, against humanity, against religion, in order to maintain the state. And therefore, it is needful that he have a mind so disposed that he can turn as the winds of fortune and the variations of things command him; and, as has been said above, not to depart from the good, if he is able, but to know how to enter the bad, when necessitated to do so.

A prince, then, ought to take great care that nothing goes out of his mouth which is not full of the five qualities written above, and that he appears to be, when one sees and hears him, all pity, all faith, all integrity, all humanity, and all religion. Nothing is more necessary than to have this last quality. For men, universally, judge more by the eyes than by the hands, because it is given to everyone that they see, but to few that they can touch.[5] Everyone sees what you seem to be, but few touch what you are, and those few will not dare to oppose themselves to the opinion of the many who have the majesty of the state defending them. And with respect to all human actions, and especially those of princes where there is no judge to whom to appeal, one looks to the end. Let a prince then win and maintain the state — the means will always be judged honorable and will be praised by everyone;[6] for the vulgar are always taken in by the appearance and the outcome of a thing, and in this world there is no one but the vulgar. The few have no place while the many have a great number of places upon which they may perch.[7] A certain present-day prince, whom it is not good to name,[8] never preaches anything but peace and faith, and is the greatest enemy of the one and of the other; and one as well as the other, if he had observed them, would many times have taken from him either his reputation or his state.

Notes

1. *dovete* — The courteous second person is used. See Ch. III, n. 19, above.

2. Chiron taught riding, hunting, healing, and music. He is also said to have taught Asclepius the art of healing. See *Iliad*, XI.832; Pindar *Nemea*, 3.53ff.; Plutarch, *Moralia*, 1145E.

3. On the figures of the fox and the lion, see Cicero, *Offices*, I.xiii.

4. The second person familiar is used.

5. See the Introduction for a discussion of this passage. See also the *Mandragola*, V.2.

6. This is the notorious passage often cited on the ends' justifying any means one uses. The passage, of course, does not quite say that.

7. One should imagine a bird coop where the rare and exotic birds are crowded off the perches.

8. Reputedly, Ferdinand of Spain. See Ch. XXI, below.

XIX

OF AVOIDING CONTEMPT AND HATRED*

But because I have spoken of the most important qualities mentioned above, I wish to discuss the others briefly under these generalities: that the prince should think, as has in part been said above, of avoiding those things which make him hateful and contemptible; and when he avoids this, he will have done his part and he will find no danger in the other vices. What makes him hated above all, as I said, is rapaciousness and the usurpation of the goods and the women of his subjects. He should abstain from these, for the universality of men live contentedly when neither their goods nor their honor are taken, and one then has only to combat the ambition of the few, who may be restrained in many modes and with ease. He is made contemptible by being held to be changeable, light, effeminate, pusillanimous, irresolute, and from these the prince ought to guard himself as from a reef, and to contrive that in his actions one will recognize greatness, spiritedness, gravity, strength. As for the private affairs of his subjects, he should will that his judgment be irrevocable, and see to it that he maintains such an opinion of [his firmness], that no one thinks of deceiving him or of getting around him.

*De Contemptu et Odio Fugiendo.

The prince who maintains such an opinion about himself will be much reputed; and one conspires with difficulty against one who has such a reputation — he will be attacked with difficulty, provided it is understood that he is an excellent man and is revered by his own. For a prince ought to have two fears: one fear arises from within and concerns his subjects; the other arises from without and concerns external powers. One defends oneself from the latter fear with good arms and good friends, and if one has good arms, one will always have good friends; and internal affairs will be stable if external affairs are stable, provided that the former have not already been disturbed by conspiracy. And even if external affairs are in motion, if a prince has so ordered himself and has lived as I have said, and if he does not falter, he will always sustain every attack, as I said Nabis the Spartan did.[1]

But concerning his subjects, if external affairs are not in motion, he has to fear that they may secretly conspire and from this the prince secures himself sufficiently by avoiding becoming hated or despised, and in keeping the people satisfied with him; all of which is necessary for him to do as has been said above at length. And one of the most potent remedies a prince has against conspiracies is not to be hated by the universality [of mankind], because he who conspires always believes that the death of the prince will satisfy the people; but if he instead believes that it will offend them, then he will not be able to pluck up his courage to take such a part, for the difficulties on the part of conspirators are infinite. And one sees by experience that there have been many conspiracies, and few have come to a good end because a conspirator cannot act alone, and he can get companions only from those whom he believes are malcontents; and upon your[2] discovering your mind to one who is a malcontent, you immediately give him the matter whereby he may become content, for by revealing the conspiracy he can hope that every advantage may be his; such that, seeing the certain gain on this side, and seeing how dubious and full of danger is the other, one needs must be a rare friend indeed, or else one must be wholly an obstinate enemy of the prince if he is to keep faith with you.

And to reduce this to brief terms, I say that on the part of the conspirator there is nothing but fear, jealousy, and the anticipation of punishment which terrifies him; but on the part of the prince there is the majesty of the principate, the laws, the protection of friends and the state, all of which defend him; such that joining popular good will to all these things, it is impossible that anyone be so bold as to conspire. And where ordinarily a conspirator must fear before the execution of his evil, in this case he must also fear what will follow from the excess (having the people for an enemy), and because of this he cannot hope to find any refuge.

One could give infinite examples of this matter, but I shall content myself with only one which occurred within the memory of our fathers. Messer Annibale Bentivoglio, prince of Bologna and grandfather of the present Annibale, was killed by the Canneschi, who had conspired against him, and no one remained of his [house], except Messer Giovanni, who was in swaddling clothes. Immediately after that homicide, the people rose up and killed all the Canneschi. That act proceeded from the popular goodwill which the house of Bentivogli had in those times; such that, no one of that [house] remaining in Bologna who could rule the state with Annibale dead, and having an indication that there was in Florence one born of the Bentivogli who had until then been taken to be the son of a blacksmith, the Bolognese came to him in Florence, and gave him the government of their city — it was governed by him until Messer Giovanni became of age to govern.[3]

I conclude, therefore, that a prince ought to take little account of conspirators when he has the goodwill of the people; but when they are his enemies and bear him hatred, he ought to fear everything and everyone. And well-ordered states and wise princes have with all diligence thought of not making the great desperate, and of satisfying the people and keeping them content;

for this is one of the most important matters that belongs to a prince.

Among the kingdoms in our times which are well-ordered and governed is that of France: and in it are to be found infinite good institutions upon which depend the liberty and security of the king. The first of these is the Parliament and its authority; for he who ordered that kingdom,[4] knowing the ambition of the powerful and their insolence, and judging it necessary that they have a bit in their mouths to correct them and, on the other hand, knowing the hatred which is founded on fear by the universality [of men] for the great, and wishing to reassure them,[5] he did not want that this should be a particular concern of the king and he sought to remove from himself any blame which he would receive from the great if he favored the people, or from the people if he favored the great, and he therefore constituted a third judge who would keep down the great and favor the small without placing any burden upon the king. Nor could there be anything better than this ordinance, nor more prudent, nor was there a greater cause of the security of the king and of the kingdom. Whence one may draw something else which is noteworthy: that princes ought to let burdensome things be administered by others, and keep for themselves those which are of grace and favor. Anew, I conclude that a prince ought to esteem the great, but not make himself hated by the people.

It might perhaps appear to many, considering the life and death of some Roman emperor, that there might be examples contrary to my opinion; for they find someone who has always lived excellently and shown great virtue of mind and who, nevertheless, lost the imperium, or was even murdered by his own who conspired against him. Wishing, therefore, to respond to these objections, I shall discuss the qualities of some emperors, showing the causes of their ruin, which are not different from those which have been adduced by me; and in part I shall put in considerations of those things which are notable for him who reads the actions of those times. And I wish to let it suffice to take those emperors who succeeded to the imperium from Marcus the philosopher to Maximinus: these were Marcus, his son Commodus, Pertinax, Julianus, Severus, his son Antoninus Caracalla, Macrinus, Heliogabalus, Alexander and Maximinus.[6]

And it is to be noted first that whereas in other principates one has only to contend with the ambition of the great and the insolence of the people, the Roman emperors had a third difficulty: that of having to bear with the cruelty and avarice of the soldiers. This was so difficult that it was the cause of the ruin of many, since it was difficult to satisfy the soldiers and the people; for the people loved quiet and therefore loved modest princes, and the soldiers loved the prince of warlike mind and one who was insolent, cruel and rapacious; which things they wanted him to practise upon the people, in order to be able to double their stipends and give vent to their avarice and cruelty.

These things made it such that those emperors were always ruined who, by nature or by art, did not have a great reputation, such that they could hold in rein the soldiers and the people; and most of them, especially those who came as new men to the principate, knowing the difficulty of these two diverse humors, turned to satisfying the soldiers, caring little about injuring the people. The choice was necessary, for if princes are not able to escape from being hated by someone, they ought first try not to be hated by the general body,[7] and when they are not able to achieve this, they ought to contrive with all industry to avoid the hatred of those bodies that are the most powerful. And therefore those emperors, who because of their newness had need of extraordinary favors, adhered to the soldiers rather than to the people; and this, nevertheless, turned out for them to be useful or not according to whether that prince knew how to maintain his reputation with them.

From these above-mentioned causes it proceeded that Marcus, Pertinax and Alexander, being all of modest life, lovers of justice, enemies of cruelty, human, benign, all, except for Marcus, came to a sad end. Marcus alone lived and died exceedingly honored, because he succeeded to the imperium by hereditary right, and he did not have to acknowledge receiving it either from the soldiers or from the people; moreover, being accompanied by many virtues which made him venerated, he was always able while he lived to keep in order one of the factions while the other was kept within limits, and he was never hated or despised. But Pertinax was created Emperor against the will of the soldiers who because they were used to living licentiously under Commodus could not bear that honest life to which Pertinax wished to recall them; and having created hatred for himself (and to this hatred there was added contempt for old age), he was ruined at the very beginning of his administration.

And here one ought to note that hatred is acquired by good works as well as evil ones — and therefore, as I said above, a prince who wants to maintain the state is often forced to be not good; when that body which you[8] choose to maintain you because you have the need is corrupt, whether it be the people or the soldiers or the great, you must follow their humor to satisfy them — and then good works are your enemies. But let us come to Alexander, who had so much goodness that among other praises that are attributed to him is this one: that during the fourteen years that he had the imperium, no one was ever put to death without trial; nevertheless, since he was held to be effeminate and a man who let himself be governed by his mother, and he came to be despised because of this, the army conspired against him and killed him.

Discussing now, in contrast, the qualities of Commodus, Severus, Antoninus Caracalla and Maximinus, you[9] will find them exceedingly cruel and rapacious; in order to satisfy the soldiers, they did not fail to inflict upon the people every kind of injury, and all of them, except Severus, ended badly. For in Severus there was so much virtue that, maintaining the soldiers friendly, even though the people were burdened by him, he was always able to rule happily; for his virtues made him so wonderful in the view of the soldiers and of the people that the former remained, in a certain way, astonished and stupefied, and the others reverent and satisfied. And because the actions of that man were so great and notable in a new prince, I would like to show briefly how well he knew how to use the *persona* of the fox and that of the lion; which are the natures I said above are necessary for a prince to imitate.

Severus knew of the indolence of Emperor Julianus; he persuaded his army, of which he was the captain in Slavonia, that it would be good to go to Rome to avenge the death of Pertinax, whom the praetorian guard had killed. Under this color, without showing any aspiration for the imperium, he moved his army against Rome and was in Italy before his departure was known. After his arrival in Rome, he was elected Emperor by the Senate through fear, and Julianus was murdered. After this beginning there remained two difficulties for Severus if he wished to make himself the master of the whole state: one in Asia, where Pescennius Niger, head of the Asiatic armies, had had himself called Emperor; the other in the west, where there was Albinus who also aspired to the imperium. Because he judged it dangerous to discover himself an enemy to both at once, he decided to attack Niger and to deceive Albinus. He wrote the latter that, since he had been elected Emperor by the Senate, he wanted to share this dignity with him, and he sent him the title of Caesar, and took him as a colleague by the resolution of the Senate. These things were accepted by Albinus as the truth. But after Severus had conquered and murdered Niger, and pacified affairs in the East, he returned to Rome and complained to the Senate that Albinus, little recognizing the benefits received from him, had treacherously sought to kill him, and that he was necessitated to go and punish this ingratitude. He then went to find him in France, and took from him his state and his life.

He who will examine in detail, then, the actions of this man, will find him a most ferocious lion and a most astute fox; he will see him feared and revered by everyone and not hated by the armies; and one will not wonder that he, a new man, was able to keep so much imperium, for his very great reputation always protected him from that hatred which the people might have conceived because of his rapacity. But Antoninus, his son, was also a man of most excellent parts who made himself marvelous in the view of the people and pleasing to the soldiers; for he was a warlike man, exceedingly able to endure every toil, he scorned all delicate food and all softness — and this made him loved by all of the armies. Nevertheless, his ferocity and cruelty were so great and so unheard of, by having, after infinite individual slayings, murdered a great part of the people of Rome and all those of Alexandria, that he became extremely hateful to all the world. And he began to be feared also by those he had around him, in such a mode that he was killed by a centurion in the midst of his army.

Whence it is to be noted that murders such as these, which follow from the deliberation of an obstinate mind, are unavoidable for princes; for anyone who does not care about dying can do him harm; but since such cases are extremely rare, it is well for the prince to have little fear of them. He ought only to guard against not doing grave injury to anyone who serves him, or those whom he has around him in the service of the principate — as Antoninus had done, who had murdered, in a disgraceful way, a brother of that centurion, and then also threatened the man himself daily, while still keeping him as a body-guard; and it was a rash policy and such as to bring ruin, as happened to him.

But let us come to Commodus, for whom it was very easy to keep the imperium, who as the son of Marcus had it by hereditary right; and it would have sufficed for him only to have followed in the footsteps of his father to satisfy the soldiers and the people. But since he had a cruel and bestial mind, in order to practise his rapacity on the people, he turned to indulging the armies and making them licentious; and, on the other hand, in not keeping his dignity, descending often into the theater to fight with gladiators, and doing other things most base and little worthy of imperial majesty, he became contemptible in the sight of the soldiers. And since he was hated on the one hand and despised on the other, he was conspired against and murdered.

There remains to narrate the qualities of Maximinus. He was an exceedingly bellicose man, and since the armies were wearied with the softness of Alexander, which I have discussed above, murdering him, they elected Maximinus to the imperium. He did not long possess it because two things made him hated and contemptible: one, the extreme baseness [of his origin]; he formerly herded sheep in Thrace (this was very well-known to all, and made him greatly despised in the sight of everyone); the other, his having deferred going to Rome to take possession of the imperial seat at the beginning of his principate, and he gained for himself the opinion that he was exceedingly cruel, having through his prefects, in Rome and in every other part of the empire, practised many cruelties. Such that, the whole world moved by disdain for the baseness of his blood, and the hatred which arose from fear of his ferocity, Africa rebelled first, and then the Senate with all the people of Rome; and all of Italy conspired against him. His own army joined these. It was besieging Aquileia and finding it difficult to conquer; disgusted with his cruelty, and seeing that he had so many enemies, it came to fear him less and killed him.

I do not wish to reason about either Heliogabalus or Macrinus or Julianus who, by being wholly contemptible, were immediately extinguished; but I shall come to the conclusion of this discourse. And I say that the princes of our times have less of this difficulty of satisfying the excessive demands of the soldiers in their government; because, notwithstanding that they have to show them some consideration, yet the difficulty is quickly resolved, for none of these princes has armies which are altogether deeply-rooted in the government and administration of the provinces, as were the armies of the Roman Empire. And therefore, if it was necessary then to satisfy the soldiers more than the people, it was because the soldiers could do more than the people; now it is more necessary for all princes, except the Turk and the Sultan,[10] to satisfy the people rather than the soldiers, because the people can do more than these.

I make an exception of the Turk, since he always keeps around him twelve thousand infantry and fifteen thousand horse, on whom depend the security and strength of his kingdom; and it is necessary, postponing every other concern, that the lord keep them friendly. So too is the kingdom of the Sultan wholly in the hands of soldiers, and it needs must be also that he, without concern for the people, keep the soldiers friendly. And you[11] have to note that this state of the Sultan is different from all other principates, because it is similar to the Christian pontificate, which one cannot call either a hereditary principate or a new principate; for it is not the sons of the old prince who are the heirs and remain the lords, but he who is elected to that rank by those who have authority. And since this order is ancient, one cannot call it a new principate, for one finds therein none of those difficulties that new ones have; for although the prince is new, the orders of that state are old and ordained to receive him as if he were their hereditary lord.

But let us return to our matter.[12] I say that whosoever will consider the discourse written above will see that either hatred or disdain was the cause of the ruin of the emperors named above; and he will also know how it came about that although part of them proceeded in one mode and part in the contrary, whichever mode they proceeded in, that one of them came to a happy and the others to an unhappy end. For Pertinax and Alexander, since they were new princes, it was useless and harmful to wish to imitate Marcus, who came to the principate by hereditary right; and similarly for Caracalla, Commodus and Maximinus, it was a very pernicious thing to imitate Severus, since they did not have sufficient virtue to follow in his footsteps. Therefore a new prince in a new principate, cannot imitate the actions of Marcus, nor is it even necessary to follow those of Severus; but he ought to take from Severus those parts which are necessary to found his state, and from Marcus those which are fitting and glorious to preserve a state which is already established and firm.

Notes

1. See Chapter IX, above.

2. The second person familiar is used. But the "tu" no longer refers to the prince but to the conspirator.

3. Annibale Bentivoglio was killed in 1445, and Santi Bentivoglio, the presumed natural son of the cousin of Annibale Bentivoglio, ruled until 1462, when Giovanni came of age. *Florentine Histories*, VI.9-10.

In the account given in the *Florentine Histories*, what emerges is the credulity of the people, their deep desire, brought about by a jealous factionalism, to have, however slim, a connection to the blood to which they had become accustomed. Machiavelli remarks that Santi was "not only honored, but almost adored."

4. Charlemagne (742-814); see *Discourses*, I.16 and note 7 by Walker, in Vol. II, p. 41. The *Parlement* of Paris was the court, in Carolingian times, in which the higher nobility were tried. See also *Discourses*, III.1.

5. There seems to be an ambiguity as to who is to be reassured, the people or the great.

6. Marcus Aurelius reigned from 161 to 180. Marcus Commodus was assassinated in 193 by Marcia, his mistress, and Laetus, the praetorian prefect. Publius Helvius Pertinax was Emperor from January to March of 193. Marcus Didius Julianus bought the Empire, March 28, 193, from the Praetorian Guard in a mock auction, and was murdered June 1, 193. Lucius Septimius Severus was

acclaimed as Emperor on April 13, 193, and died a natural death in 211. Marcus Aurelius Antoninus Caracalla was assassinated in 217. Marcus Opellius Macrinus was the praetorian prefect who assassinated Antoninus Caracalla out of fear — he was put to death in 218. Heliogabalus, born Varius Avitus Bassianus, was a hereditary priest of the sun-god of Emesa, Elah-Gabal — he was assassinated in 222. Marcus Aurelius Severus Alexander, the reign name of Alexianus, was only 13 on his accession and was always therefore under the influence of his mother, Julia Mamaea — he was assassinated in 235. Caius Julius Verus Maximinus was assassinated in 238.

Chapter XIX is the longest chapter in the *Prince*; and the longest chapter in the *Discourses* is III.6 which also treats of conspiracies. But the direct discussion of conspiracies is relatively brief here, as it probably must be in a book addressed to princes, who are necessarily a little tender about such things. The rest of the chapter attempts to answer the objection which a reader might raise, that a prince of great virtue does not always securely establish himself. The issue seems to be the power of chance, and the weakness of virtue. The example of a virtuous man, overcome by chance, would seem to be best found among the Roman emperors, and the rest of the chapter is a review of the succession to the imperium of Rome from A.D. 161 to 238.

Machiavelli does not say here why he chooses to discuss this particular period in Roman history. But in the *Discourses,* I.10 he tells us that the reign of Marcus Aurelius was the close of the golden age of the Empire:

> Let us place then, before a prince, the times from Nerva to Marcus, and let him compare them with those which came before and then afterwards; and then let him choose in which he would have wished to be born, or in which he would wish to be placed. For, in these governments of the good, he will see a prince secure in the midst of his secure citizenry; the world replete with peace and justice: he will see the Senate with authority, the magistrates honored; rich citizens

enjoying their riches; nobility and virtue exalted: he will see every quiet and every good; and on the other side, every rancor, every license, corruption and ambition extinguished; he will see the golden age where everyone can hold and defend whatever opinions he wills. He will see, in fine, the world triumphant; the prince overflowing with glory and reverence, the people with love and security.

The period with which Chapter XIX is concerned is therefore that which immediately follows the best age of the Empire. Machiavelli is silent upon one of the most important aspects of this period. Gibbon describes it as follows:

By a singular fatality, the hardships which they [the Christians] had endured under the government of a virtuous prince immediately ceased on the accession of a tyrant; and as none except themselves had experienced the injustice of Marcus [Aurelius], so they alone were protected by the lenity of Commodus. The celebrated Marcia, the most favored of his concubines, and who at length contrived the murder of her Imperial lover, entertained a singular affection for the oppressed church; and although it was impossible that she could reconcile the practice of vice with the precepts of the Gospel, she might hope to atone for the frailties of her sex and profession by declaring herself the patroness of the Christians. Under the gracious protection of Marcia they passed in safety the thirteen years of a cruel tyranny; and when the empire was established in the house of Severus, they formed a domestic but more honorable connection with the new court. The emperor was persuaded that, in a dangerous sickness, he had derived some benefit, either spiritual or physical, from the holy oil which one of his slaves had anointed him. He always treated with peculiar distinction several persons of both sexes who had embraced the new religion. The nurse as well as the precep-tor of Caracalla were Christians; and if that young prince ever betrayed a sentiment of humanity, it was occasioned by an incident which, however, trifling, bore some relation to the cause of Christianity . . . (Vol. I, Ch. XVI, Modern Library edition, pp. 478-479).

Gibbon goes on to relate the attraction of the Empress Julia Avita Mamaea and her son Alexander to Christianity. Maximinus, in extirpating Alexander's supporters, accidentally and briefly persecuted the Christians. But the story of Christianity from this time on, despite the severe persecutions of Diocletian and some other emperors afterwards, is one of steady progress. One wonders, therefore, if Machiavelli chose this period to discuss because he "who reads the actions of those times" would know that it was during those times that Christianity first gained an influence over the minds of the rulers of the Empire.

7. *università* — the whole, or all things, and therefore, by extension, the body of the people; but it also means any body of persons treated as a unity in law, as is, for example, a guild or corporation. See Ch. XXI, n. 10, below.

8. The second person familiar is used. See Ch. VI, n. 1, above.

9. *troverrete* — The courteous second person is used. See Ch. III, n. 19, above.

10. The Sultan is the Sultan of Egypt, which was then ruled by the Mamelukes. The Turk possibly refers to Selim I (1465-1520). Selim I marched on Egypt and annexed it to the Ottoman Empire in 1517. The state of the Sultan is that of the caliphate, the spiritual authority of Islam, which Selim took over, thus combining in the person of the Turkish sultan both temporal power and spiritual authority. Selim I is praised in the *Discourses,* I.19, where the context is that of the difficulties in providing for the succession.

The comparison between the caliphate and the pontificate leads inevitably to the question of whether or not it is possible for the pontificate to become like the caliphate, especially after the enterprises of the Borgias and Julius II which gave the Church temporal power. See Ch. XI, above, and especially the *Florentine Histories* I.23 - end.

11. *avete* — The courteous second person is used.

12. On the significance of Machiavelli's digressions, see Strauss, *Thoughts on Machiavelli,* pp. 47-49.

XX

IF FORTRESSES AND MANY OTHER THINGS WHICH EVERYDAY ARE EMPLOYED BY PRINCES ARE USEFUL OR USELESS*

Some princes, in order to keep the state securely, have disarmed their subjects; some others have kept their subject towns divided; some have nourished enmities against themselves; some others have turned to gaining to themselves those who were suspect at the beginning of their state; some have built fortresses; some have ruined and destroyed them. And even though one cannot give a definite judgment upon all these things without coming to the particular circumstances of those states where one might have to make some such similar deliberations, I shall speak, nevertheless, in as general a mode as the matter in itself supports.

There has never been, then, a new prince who has disarmed his subjects; on the contrary, when he has found them disarmed, he has always armed them, because, in arming them, those arms become yours;[1] those whom you suspected become faithful; and those who were faithful are kept so, and as for the subjects, they are made your partisans. Since all the subjects cannot be armed, when those whom you arm are benefited, you can then better secure yourself with the others, for they [whom you arm]

An Arces et Multa Alia Quae Cotidie a Principibus Fiunt Utilia an Inutilia Sint.

recognize that [you] proceed with them differently, and this makes them obligated to you; the others excuse you, judging it necessary that those who undergo more dangers and more obligations should have more merit. But when you disarm them, you begin to offend them, for you show that you distrust them either from cowardice or from lack of faith — and the one and the other of these opinions gives birth to hatred against you. And since you cannot be disarmed, it needs must be that you turn to mercenary militia, which is of that quality mentioned above;[2] and even if these might be good, they cannot defend you from powerful enemies and untrustworthy subjects.

Therefore, as I have said, a new prince in a new principate has always ordered arms in it; and the histories are full of examples of these. But when a prince acquires a new state which as a member is joined to his old one, then it is necessary to disarm that state, except for those who were your partisans in its acquisition; and it is necessary to render even those soft and effeminate with time and with the occasion, and to order them in such a mode that the arms of your whole state be only those of your own soldiers, who lived close to you in your old state.

Our ancestors and old men, and those who are esteemed wise, used to say that it was necessary to hold Pistoia with factions and Pisa with fortresses; and because of this they nourished differences in some subject town of theirs in order to possess it more easily.[3] This might have been good to do in those times when Italy was balanced in a certain mode, but I do not believe that one can give that as a precept today, because I do not believe that divisions ever do anyone any good; on the contrary, it is necessary when the enemy accosts it that the divided city will be lost immediately, for the weaker party will always adhere to the forces outside, and the other will not be able to stand.

The Venetians, moved, as I believe, by the reasons written above, nourished the Guelf and Ghibelline sects[4] in their subject cities; and although they never let them come to blood, still they

nourished among them such dissensions that those citizens, occupied by their differences, might not unite against them. This, as
has been seen, did not afterwards turn out according to plan, for,
being defeated at Vailà, immediately one part among these
became bold, and took away all their state.[5] Such modes argue,
besides, the weakness of the prince, for in a vigorous principate
such divisions would never be permitted; because they are
profitable only in time of peace, enabling one, by means of them,
more easily to manage the subjects; but when war comes, such
a policy shows its weakness.

Without doubt princes become great when they overcome the
difficulties and the opposition which are made theirs; and
therefore fortune,[6] especially when she wishes to make great a
new prince, who has greater necessity of acquiring reputation
than a hereditary one, makes enemies for him and brings
enterprises against him so that he may have cause to surpass them
and climb higher on the ladder his enemies bring him. Therefore
many judge that a wise prince should, when he has the occasion,
nourish with cunning some enmities, so that, crushing them, the
result is the increase of his greatness.

Princes, and especially those who are new, have found more
faith and more utility in those men whom they suspected at the
beginning of their state, than in those of whom they were confident from the beginning. Pandolfo Petrucci, prince of Siena,[7]
ruled his state more with those who were suspected by him than
with others. But one cannot speak at large of this matter, because
it varies according to the subject. I shall only say this, that the
prince with great ease can always gain those men, who in the
beginning of a principate were enemies, if they are of such quality
that to maintain themselves they have need of support; the prince
will always with the greatest facility be able to win them over, and
they are all the more forced to serve him faithfully, for they know
that it is necessary for them to cancel with deeds the adverse opinion that he has of them. And therefore the prince always finds

them more useful than those who, in serving him with too much security, neglect his affairs.

And since the matter requires it, I do not wish to omit reminding princes who have newly taken a state by means of the favors of those within, to consider well what cause may have moved those who favored him to favor him; and if it is not a natural affection for him, but only because they were not content with that state, then with toil and great difficulty will he be able to keep them his friends, for it is impossible that he make them content. And discussing well the cause of this, with examples taken from ancient and modern things, he will see that it is much easier to gain as his friends those men who were content with the former state, although they were his enemies, than those who became his friends by not being content and favored him in seizing it.

It has been the custom of princes in order to keep their state more securely, to build fortresses, which served as the bridle and the bit for those who might plot against them, and provided a refuge secure from a sudden onset.[8] I praise this mode because it has been used from antiquity. Nevertheless, in our times, Messer Niccolò Vitelli was seen destroying two fortresses in Città di Castello, in order to keep that state. Guido Ubaldo, Duke of Urbino,[9] returning to his domains whence Cesare Borgia had driven him, razed all the fortresses of that province to their foundations, judging that without them he would with more difficulty lose that state again. The Bentivogli, when they returned to Bologna, took similar measures. Fortresses, then, are useful or not according to the times; and if they do good for you[10] in one part, they harm you in another. And one may discuss this part as follows.

That prince who fears the people more than foreigners, ought to build fortresses; but he who fears foreigners more than the people should leave them behind. The castle of Milan, built by Francesco Sforza, has made and will make more war against the Sforzesca house than any other disorder in that state. Therefore not to be hated by the people is the best fortress there is; for, even if you have fortresses, they will not save you if the people hold you in hatred; for the people, as soon as they have arms, will never lack foreigners to help them. In our times, one has not seen fortresses to have profited any prince, except the Countess of Forlì, when Girolamo, her consort, died; for, by means of them, she was able to escape the popular rebellion, await the help of Milan and recover the state.[11] And the times stood then in such a mode that the foreigner was not able to help the people. But then again, afterwards, fortresses were of small value when Cesare Borgia assaulted her; and since the people were her enemies they joined with the foreigner. Therefore, then and at first, it would have been safer for her not to be hated by the people than to have had fortresses. Having considered, then, all these things, I shall praise him who will build fortresses and him who will not build them; and I shall blame anyone who, trusting in fortresses, will esteem little being hated by the people.

Notes

1. The second person familiar is used. See Ch. VI, n.1, above.

2. See Ch. XII, above.

3. See also *Discourses,* III.27.

4. See Ch. XII, n. 19, above.

5. Brescia and Verona, and then Vincenza and Padua, were briefly in rebellion after Vailà. For the battle of Vailà, see Ch. XII, n. 17, above.

6. This is the first mention of fortune as a willing and acting being.

7. Pandolfo Petrucci was lord of Siena from 1500 to 1512. See *Discourses,* III.6.

8. On fortresses, see *Discourses,* II.24; III.27.

9. Guido Ubaldo of Montefeltro, son of the famed Federigo, was

one of the most noted of the *condottieri,* but his reputation was based upon his father's and not his own deeds. He was driven out of Urbino without a shot being fired; regained the city after the Diet of Magione (see Ch. VII, above), and then was driven out again. He returned after the death of Alexander VI.

10. The second person familiar is used.

11. Girolamo Riario was assassinated in 1488. See *Discourses,* III.6, and *Florentine Histories,* VIII.34.

XXI

WHAT A PRINCE SHOULD DO
THAT HE MAY BE ESTEEMED*

Nothing makes a prince so esteemed as when he does great enterprises and gives of himself rare examples.[1] We have in our times Ferdinand of Aragon, the present King of Spain[2] One can almost call that man a new prince, because from a weak king he became by fame and glory the first king of the Christians; and if you[3] will consider his actions, you will find them all extremely great and some of them extraordinary. In the beginning of his reign he attacked Granada, and that enterprise was the foundation of his state. He did it leisurely and without any fear of being impeded;[4] he kept occupied the minds of the barons of Castile thereby, who did not think about making innovations because they were thinking of the war. And he acquired, by that means, reputation and imperium over them, of which they perceived nothing. He was able with the money of the Church and of the people to support armies and establish a foundation for his militia with that long war, which afterwards gave honor to him. Besides this, in order to undertake greater enterprises, always serving religion, he turned to a pious cruelty, driving out of his kingdom and despoiling the Marranos — and there cannot be a

Quod Principem Deceat ut Egregius Habeatur.

132

more miserable and rare example than this.[5] He assaulted Africa under this same cloak; he made the enterprise of Italy; he has finally assaulted France. He has thus always done and ordered great things, which have always kept the minds of his subjects in suspense and admiration and occupied them with their outcome. And these actions of his arose one from the other, in such a mode, that he never gave space to men, between the one and the other, to work quietly against him.

It is also very useful for a prince to give rare examples by himself with respect to his government within, similar to those which are narrated of Messer Bernabò of Milan;[6] when the opportunity is given him of someone who does some extraordinary thing in civil life, whether good or bad, he should pick a mode, with respect to rewarding and punishing him, of which much will be said. And above all, a prince ought to contrive by every action of his to give himself the fame of being a great man and one of excellent ingenuity.

And a prince is also esteemed when he is a true friend and a true enemy; that is, when, without any respect, he discloses himself in favor of someone against another. This part is always more useful than to be neutral, for if two of your[7] neighboring powers come to blows they will be of such quality that, when one of these wins, you will either have to fear the victor or you will not. And in either of these cases it will always be more useful for you to disclose yourself and wage a good war; for, in the first case, if you do not disclose yourself you will always be the prey of the victor, with the pleasure and satisfaction of the one who has been conquered; you will have no excuse nor anything else which can defend you and no one to receive you; for the victor will not want to have suspect friends who did not aid him in adversity; and he who lost will not receive you, because you did not want to risk his fortune with arms in hand.

When Antiochus had passed into Greece, brought there by the Aetolians to drive out the Romans, he sent ambassadors to the

Achaeans who were friends of the Romans, to induce them to stand in the middle; and on the other side the Romans were persuading [the Achaeans] to take up arms for them. This matter came up for deliberation in the council of the Achaeans, where the legate of Antiochus persuaded them to be neutrals — to which the Roman legate responded: "What these say about not interposing yourselves in the war, nothing is more alien to your affairs; without thanks, without dignity, the prize of the victors will you be."[8]

And it will always happen that he who is not a friend will seek after your neutrality, and he who is a friend will seek after you to disclose yourself with arms. And irresolute princes, in order to avoid present dangers, most of the time follow the road of neutrality, and most of the time they are ruined. But when a prince discloses himself boldly in favor of one party, if that one to whom you have adhered wins, even though he may be powerful and you remain at his discretion, he has been obliged to you, and there is a contract of love; and men are never so dishonest, that with such an example of ingratitude they would oppress you; moreover, victories are never so clear that the victor does not have to have some respect, and especially for justice.[9] But if that one to whom you have adhered loses, you are received by him; and while he can he aids you, and you become the companion of a fortune which can rise again. In the second case, when those who fight each other are of such quality that you do not have to fear the victor, so much more is it prudence to adhere yourself to him, because you go to the ruin of one with the aid of that one who should have saved him, were he wise; and in winning, he yet remains at your discretion, and it is impossible that he should not win with your aid.

And here it is to be noted that a prince ought to be careful never to join with one more powerful than he, in order to attack others, except when necessity constrains him, as has been said above; for, in winning, you remain his prisoner; and princes ought to avoid, as much as they can, being left at the discretion of others. The Venetians joined with France against the Duke of Milan, although they could have avoided making that alliance, which resulted in their ruin. But when it cannot be avoided (as happened to the Florentines when the Pope and Spain went with their armies to assault Lombardy), then the prince ought to adhere for the above-mentioned reasons. Nor let any state ever believe that it is always able to pick a part safely, rather let it think of having to take all as dubious; for one finds this in the order of things, that one never seeks to avoid an inconvenience without running into another; but prudence consists in knowing how to recognize the qualities of inconveniences and to pick the less bad as good.

A prince should also show himself a lover of virtue, giving welcome to virtuous men, and honoring the excellent in an art. Next, he should encourage his citizens, enabling them quietly to practise their trades in merchandise and in agriculture and in every other trade of men — so that this one is not afraid to embellish his possessions for fear that these might be taken from him, nor this other to open a traffic for fear of taxes. But he ought to prepare rewards for the one who wants to do these things, and for whoever thinks, in whatever mode, of increasing his city or his state. He should, besides this, at the proper times of the year, keep the people occupied with feasts and spectacles. And because every city is divided into arts and trades, he should take account of these universities,[10] meeting with them sometimes, and making himself an example of humanity and munificence, always keeping firmly, nevertheless, the majesty of his dignity, for this he does not want to be lacking in anything.

Notes

1. *dare di sé rari esempli* — "to give by (and of) himself rare examples." By "rare examples" Machiavelli seems to mean examples of one's character of which much will be said; and which, above

all, will astonish and satisfy the people, as Cesare Borgia did when
he cut Remirro de Orco into two pieces (Ch. VII). A rare example
is one which is unexpected, seemingly unimaginable and, above
all, spectacular. As it becomes clear subsequently, when he refers
to Bernabò Visconti of Milan, he has executions chiefly in mind.
As it also becomes clear, a rare example is not necessarily a virtuous action, in the sense in which Machiavelli uses *virtù,* that is,
bespeaking greatness of mind and body (Ch. VIII). It may be a
"miserable" action as was, for example, Ferdinand's exiling of the
Marranos, but it is one which will occupy men's minds in wonder
and suspense, awaiting the next unheard of but thrilling deed.
Machiavelli fully understood the popular appetite for the spectacular or the circus.

2. Ferdinand (1452-1516), II of Aragon, and V of Castile (1474-
1504), also called Ferdinand the Catholic. He finally forced the
surrender of Granada in 1492; in 1509, he sent an expedition to
Oran, continuing the Crusade against the Muslims; from 1493 he
turned his attention to Aragonese affairs in Italy, first taking Sicily
from the French in 1496 and then all of the Kingdom of Naples
from Louis XII of France in 1504; together with the Pope, the
Venetians, and the Swiss mercenaries, he drove the French from
Italy in 1511-1513; and, finally, he took Navarre from the French
in 1515. See *Discourses,* I.29, 40, 55; II.22; III.6.

3. *considerrete, troverrete* — The courteous second person is
used. See Ch. III, n. 19, above.

4. *e la fece ozioso e sanza sospetto di essere impedito* — The
usual translation of this phrase is: "he did it when he was at peace,
and was without fear of being impeded." But it seems to me that
the context makes it clear that he proceeded slowly so as not to
awaken the suspicions of the barons, who did not perceive his
policy of acquiring power over them by means of the war, until it
was too late.

5. The Marranos were converted Jews who were accused of prac-

tising Judaism in secret while publicly professing Christianity. The Jews and the Marranos were expelled from Spain in 1501-1502.

6. Bernabò Visconti was Duke of Milan from 1354 to 1385. He was notorious for his extraordinary modes of punishment.

7. The second person familiar is used.

8. *Quod autem isti dicunt non interponendi vos bello, nihil magis alienum rebus vestris est; sine gratia, sine dignitate, praemium victoris eritis.* — Livy, *Histories,* XXXV.49.

9. One wonders, of course, about Machiavelli's concern for justice here, when he has previously told us that most men look to the end; and that the prince need only win and maintain the state and "the means will always be judged honorable" (Ch. XVIII, above).

10. *università* — The arts and trades were incorporated into guilds, associations and other bodies, which were still at that time called "universities." See Ch. XIX, n. 7, above.

XXII

OF THOSE WHOM PRINCES
HAVE AS SECRETARIES*

Of no little importance to a prince is the choice of ministers; and these are good or not, according to the prudence of the prince. The first conjecture one can make of the brain of a ruler comes from looking at the men he has around him, and when they are competent and faithful, one can always repute him to be wise because he has known how to recognize them as sufficient and to keep them faithful. But when they are otherwise, one can always come to an unfavorable judgment of him, for the first error he makes, he makes in this choice. There was no one who knew Messer Antonio da Venafro as minister of Pandolfo Petrucci, prince of Siena, who did not judge Pandolfo to be an exceedingly worthy man, for having him for his minister.

And because there are three kinds of brains: one understands on its own, the other discerns that which others understand, the third neither understands on its own nor through others; the first is most excellent, the second excellent, and the third useless; it must needs be by necessity, therefore, that if Pandolfo was not of the first rank, he was of the second: because whenever one has the judgment to know the good or evil that someone does and says,

De His Quos a Secretis Principes Habent.

though he is without invention[1] himself, he will know the minister's bad and good works, and he will extol the latter and correct the former; and the minister cannot hope to deceive him and thus keeps himself good.

But so that the prince might be able to know the minister, there is this mode which never fails: when you see the minister thinking more of himself than of you,[2] and he seeks in all actions his own interest — one so fashioned never makes a good minister; never will you be able to trust him — for he who has the state of one in hand ought never to think about himself, but only about the prince, and should never remember a thing which does not appertain to him. And on the other side, the prince, in order to keep him good, ought to think about the minister, honoring him, making him rich, obligating him to himself, sharing with him honors and burdens; so that he might see that he is not able to stand without the prince, and that his many honors not make him desire more honors, his many riches not make him desire more riches, his many burdens make him fear changes. If, then, ministers and princes, [upon this point] concerning ministers,[3] are so disposed one to another, they can have confidence in one another; but when it is otherwise, the end is always harmful for the one or the other.

Notes

1. *invenzione* — "Invention," in the now archaic sense of the capacity to discover things for oneself.

2. The second person familiar is used.

3. That is, on the point concerning "the mode which never fails" — that the prince should look for signs of disloyalty, which he ought to be intelligent enough to discern (even if the minister is someone who knows how to deceive [Ch. XVIII]), and at the same time honor, enrich and obligate the minister in such a way as to persuade him not to be disloyal.

XXIII

IN WHAT MODE FLATTERERS ARE TO BE AVOIDED*

I do not wish to omit an important heading and an error from which princes with difficulty defend themselves, if they are not most prudent, or if they do not choose well. And these are the flatterers of whom courts are full — for men are so pleased with their own things and in this mode deceive themselves that they with difficulty defend themselves from this pestilence; and the wish to defend oneself from it carries the danger of becoming contemptible. For there is no other mode of guarding oneself from flattery, except to have men understand that they will not offend you[1] by telling you the truth; but when everyone is able to tell you the truth then you lack reverence.

Therefore a prudent prince ought to take a third mode, choosing from his state wise men, and only to these ought he to give free will to speak the truth to him, but only of those things about which he asks and nothing else. But he ought to ask them about everything, and hear their opinions, and afterwards deliberate by himself, in his own mode; and with these councils, and with each one of the [counselors], he should carry himself in such a mode that everyone will recognize that the more freely he speaks, the

*Quomodo Adulatores Sint Fugiendi.

140

more will he be accepted: but outside of these, [he ought] not wish to hear anyone, [but ought] to stand behind the thing deliberated and to be unyielding in his deliberations.[2] Who does otherwise is either thrown upon the flatterers, or changes as often as opinions vary — from which it arises that he is little esteemed.

I wish on this point to adduce a modern example. Pre' Luca, a man of the present Emperor, Maximilian,[3] when speaking of his majesty said that he would not take counsel with anybody, and would not do anything according to his own mode. This arose from taking measures contrary to the ones stated above. Since the Emperor is a secretive man, he does not communicate his plans to anybody, he does not take opinions; but as they begin to be known and discovered as he puts these [plans] into effect, they begin to be contradicted by those around him, and he is very easily persuaded from them. From which it arises that those things that are done one day are destroyed the next, and no one ever understands what he wants or plans to do, and no one is able to base himself upon his deliberations.

A prince, therefore, ought always to take counsel, but only when he wishes to do so and not when others wish; indeed he ought to take the heart out of anyone counseling him on anything, when he does not ask for it. But he ought very much to be an asker-at-large, and then a patient hearer of the truth about the things asked; indeed, when he understands that someone, because of some reservation, does not speak the truth, he should be disturbed by it. Many judge that a prince who gains for himself the opinion of being a prudent man is so held not because of his nature, but because of the good counselors that he has around him — and doubtless they deceive themselves. For this is a general rule which never fails: a prince who is not wise himself cannot be well-counseled, unless by chance he consigns himself[4] to one who alone will wholly govern him and who himself is a most prudent man. In this case, he could well be, but it would not last long, for that governor[5] of his would in a short time take away the state from him. But, if he takes counsel from more than one, an unwise prince will never have unanimous counsels and he will not know by himself how to reconcile them; as for the counselors, each one will think of his own interests; and the prince will not know how to correct or understand them. And it is not possible to find it otherwise, for men always turn out badly for you unless by some necessity they are made good. It is therefore to be concluded that good counsels, from whomever they may come, needs must arise from the prudence of the prince, and not the prudence of the prince from good counsels.

Notes

1. The second person familiar is used.

2. *deliberazioni* — Deliberations, in the now somewhat archaic meaning of decisions reached as the result of deliberation.

3. Luca Rinaldi was a bishop, ambassador, and a counselor to Maximilian I (1459-1519), the Holy Roman Emperor from 1493.

4. See Ch. XIII, n. 15, above.

5. *quello governatore* — "Governor" is used here in the sense of "tutor."

XXIV

WHY THE PRINCES OF ITALY
HAVE LOST THEIR KINGDOM*

The things written above, observed prudently, make a new prince seem ancient, and immediately render him more secure and more firm in the state than if he had become ancient in it. For the actions of a new prince are much more observed than those of a hereditary one; and when they are known to be virtuous, much more do they pick up men and much more do they obligate them than does ancient blood. For men are more taken by present things than by those of the past; and when they find the good in the present, they enjoy that and seek for nothing more; on the contrary, they will take up every defense for him when he himself is not found lacking in other things. And so he will have a double glory: of beginning a new principate, and of ornamenting and strengthening it with good laws, good arms and good examples; as that one will have double shame who, though born a prince, has lost [the principate] by his little prudence.

And if one will consider those lords in Italy who have lost the state in our times, such as the King of Naples,[1] the Duke of Milan,[2] and others, one will find in them, first, a common defect as to arms, for the causes which have been discussed above at

Cur Italiae Principes Regnum Amiserunt.

143

length; moreover, one will see that some of them either made the people enemies or, if they made the people friends, they did not know how to secure themselves against the great: because, without these defects, states are not lost that have enough nerve[3] to take an army into the field.[4] Philip of Macedon,[5] not the father of Alexander but the one who was conquered by Titus Quintius, did not have much state when compared to the greatness of the Romans and of Greece who were attacking him — nevertheless, by being a military man, and one who knew how to keep and provide for the people and to secure himself against the great, he for many years sustained a war against them; and if in the end he lost the dominion of some cities, the kingdom nevertheless remained his.

Therefore, let these our princes who have been in their principate many years and then lost it not accuse fortune[6] but their own indolence; for never having in quiet times thought that [times] could change (for not to take account of the tempest during calms is a common defect of men), then when adverse times came they thought only of fleeing and never of defending themselves; and they hoped that the people, tiring of the insolence of the conquerors, would call them back. Such a remedy, when others are lacking, is good; but it is very bad indeed to have to let go other remedies for this one, for one should never fall believing that someone will be found to pick you[7] up. That either does not happen, or if it does, it is not to your security, because such a defense is base and does not depend upon you. And only those defenses are good, are certain, are durable, which depend on you yourself and on your virtue.

Notes

1. Frederick of Aragon, whose kingdom was taken by Ferdinand of Spain and Louis XII of France in 1503. See Ch. III, n. 5, above.

2. Ludovico Sforza, il Moro. See Ch. III, nn. 4 and 5, above.

3. *nervo* — Nerve, in the sense of vigor and power.

4. See Ch. X, above.

5. Philip V (237-179 B.C.), King of Macedonia (221-179 B.C.). He was defeated by the consul Titus Quintius Flamininus at Cynoscephalae in 197. Titus Quintius, noted for his philhellenism, proclaimed the freedom of Greece at the Isthmian Games in 196. He was hailed by the Greek cities as their deliverer. For Philip and Titus Quintius Flamininus, see *Discourses,* II.4, and III.10. On Philip, see also III.37.

6. See Ch. XX, n. 6, above.

7. The second person familiar is used. See Ch.VI, n.1, above.

XXV

HOW MUCH FORTUNE IS ABLE TO DO IN HUMAN THINGS AND IN WHAT MODE ONE MAY OPPOSE HER*

And it is not unknown to me how many have had and still have the opinion that because the things of the world are in a mode governed by fortune and by God, that men with their prudence are unable to correct them — indeed, that they have no remedy; and because of this they judge that it does not do to sweat much over things but to let them be governed by chance. This opinion has been believed more in our times because of the great changes in things which have been seen and may be seen every day, beyond any human conjecture. Thinking about this, I am myself sometimes and in some part inclined to their opinion.

Nevertheless, in order that our free will may not be extinguished, I judge that it could be true that fortune is the arbiter of half our actions, but that she lets the other half, or nearly that, be governed by us. And I liken her to one of those violent rivers which, when they become angry, flood the plain, destroy trees and buildings, remove the earth from one place and deposit it in another; everyone flees their advance, everybody surrenders to their impetus, unable to oppose it in any way. And although these things are so, it does not follow that men, when there are quiet

*Quantum Fortuna in Rebus Humanis Possit, et Quomodo Illi Sit Occurrendum.

146

times, cannot therefore make provisions with defenses and embankments in such a mode that, rising later, either they will go through a canal, or their impetus would not be so licentious or so harmful.

The same happens with fortune, who demonstrates her power where there is no ordered virtue to resist her; and she turns her impetus where she knows embankments and defenses to hold her have not been built. And if you[1] will consider Italy, which is the seat of these changes and the one which put them into motion, you will see her to be a country without embankments and without any defense: for, if she had been defended by the needed virtue, as were Germany, Spain and France,[2] this flood would neither have made the great changes which it has, nor would it have come. And I wish that what has been said about opposing fortune to suffice, with respect to the general.

But, restricting myself more to particulars, I say that one may see a prince happy today and ruined tomorrow, without having seen him change his nature or any quality. I believe this arises, first, from the causes which have previously been discussed at length; that is, that that prince who depends wholly upon fortune falls when she changes. I believe, then, that he is happy who finds that the mode of his procedures is at one with the qualities of the time, and similarly that he is unhappy who with his procedures is in discord with the times.

For one sees in the things which conduct them to the end that each has before him, that is to say, glory and riches, that men proceed there variously: one with circumspection, the other with impetuosity; the one by violence, the other with art; the one with patience, the other with its contrary — and each one, with these diverse modes, is able to arrive there. One might again see two cautious men: the one arrives at his purpose while the other does not. Similarly two prosper equally with two diverse plans, one being cautious and the other impetuous: all of which arises from nothing other than their procedure which does or does not conform with the quality of the times. From which arises what I have said, that two working diversely get the same effect, and of two, working similarly, one conducts himself to his end and the other does not.

Upon this does the good vary, for if one governs himself with caution and patience, and the times and circumstances turn in such a mode that his government is good, he goes on happily; but if times and circumstances change, he falls, because he does not change the mode of procedure. Nor can one find a man so prudent that he would know how to accommodate himself to this; that comes about because he is unable to deviate from that to which nature inclines him, and also because he who has always prospered walking along one way cannot be persuaded to depart from it. And therefore the cautious man, when it is time to be impetuous, does not know how to do it, whence he is ruined; for, if he changed his nature with the times and circumstances, fortune would not change.[3]

Pope Julius II[4] proceeded impetuously in every one of his affairs; and he found the times and circumstances very much in conformity with his mode of procedure, which always resulted in a happy end. Consider the first enterprise he undertook, that of Bologna, while Messer Giovanni Bentivoglio was still living.[5] The Venetians were not pleased with it; neither was the King of Spain; he was still negotiating with France over that enterprise; and nevertheless, with his ferocity and impetuosity, he personally put that expedition into motion. That motion made Spain and the Venetians stand suspended and arrested; the latter from fear, and the former from the desire to recover all the Kingdom of Naples; and, on the other side, he pulled in behind him the King of France, because the King, having seen him move and desiring to make him friendly in order to bring down the Venetians, judged that he was not able to deny the Pope his troops without manifestly offending him.

Julius conducted, then, with his impetuous motion, that which another pontiff, with all human prudence, would never have conducted: for, if he had waited to depart from Rome with the agreements firmly concluded and all things ordained, as any other pontiff would have done, he never would have succeeded; for the King of France would have had a thousand excuses and the others would have put into him a thousand fears. I wish to let stand his other actions, which are all the same, and all of which succeeded well for him. And the brevity of his life did not let him feel the contrary; for, if times had come which would have made him need to proceed with care, his ruin would have followed — he would never have deviated from those modes to which nature inclined him.

I conclude, then, that with fortune varying, and men standing obstinate in their modes, when these are in concord with each other, men are happy; and when these are in discord, unhappy. I am very much of this judgment: that it is better to be impetuous than cautious, for fortune is a woman, and if one wishes to keep her down, it is necessary to beat her and knock her down. And one sees that she lets herself be overcome more by these men than by those who proceed coldly; and therefore, like a woman, she is always a friend of the young, because they are less cautious, are fiercer, and with more audacity do they command her.[6]

Notes

1. *considerrete, vedrete* — The courteous second person is used. See Ch. III, n. 19, above.

2. Machiavelli remarks in the Preface to Book II of the *Discourses*, that virtue, in modern times, resides in France, Turkey, the caliphate, and in all the peoples of Germany. He is silent there upon virtue residing in Spain. Instead, as we have seen in Chapters XVIII and XXI, he praises the faithlessness, the ability to give rare examples, and the pious cruelty of Ferdinand.

149

The comparison of the natures of the peoples has a significance similar to the comparison of the natures of princes in Ch. XVII, n. 15, above; see also Ch. IV, n. 11, above, and *Discourses,* I.11. See also Plato, *Republic* 435e.

For the passages in the *Discourses* on the nature of France, see Ch. III, n. 5, above. For Germany and the Swiss, see Ch. X, n. 4, above. For Spain, see Ch. XXI, n.2, above. See also Strauss, *Thoughts on Machiavelli,* pp. 172, 182, and 328 (n. 192 of Ch. III).

3. See *Discourses,* III.9. See the discussion in the Introduction of these passages on the modes of men.

4. Julius II, born Giuliano della Rovere, the Cardinal San Pietro in Vincoli (1443-1513), reigned from 1503 to 1513. See *Discourses,* I.27; II.10, 24; III.9.

5. This was the first campaign of Julius II, when an astonished Christendom saw a pope act like a warrior-king. It was during this same campaign that he confronted Giovampagolo Baglioni in Perugia, for which see *Discourses,* I.27.

6. On fortune, see also *Discourses,* I.37; III.8, 9, 31, 33.

XXVI

EXHORTATION TO LAY HOLD OF ITALY AND VINDICATE HER LIBERTY FROM THE BARBARIANS*

Having considered, then, all the things discussed above, and thinking over within myself if presently in Italy the times were ready to honor a new prince, and if there was matter which could give occasion for one prudent and virtuous to introduce the form which would give honor to him and good to the general body of her men, it seems to me that so many things are concurring to benefit a new prince, that I do not know whether there ever was a time more proper than this. And if, as I have said,[1] one wished to see the virtue of Moses it was necessary that the people of Israel be enslaved in Egypt, and to know the greatness of the mind of Cyrus that the Persians be oppressed by the Medes, and [to know] the excellence of Theseus that the Athenians be dispersed — so, at present, if one wishes to know the virtue of an Italian spirit, it was necessary that Italy be reduced to her present terms, and that she be more enslaved than the Hebrews, more servile than the Persians, more dispersed than the Athenians, without head, without order, beaten, despoiled, torn asunder, overrun, and having borne every sort of ruin.

And although before this a gleam of light showed itself in a certain man, whereby one might have judged that he was ordained by

*Exhortatio Ad Capessendam Italiam in Libertatemque a Barbaris Vindicandam.

God for her redemption, yet afterwards one has seen how he was reprobated by fortune at the highest course of his actions.[2] Thus, left as if without life, in such a mode she awaits whoever will be able to heal her wounds, put an end to the plunderings of Lombardy and to the taxation of the Kingdom [of Naples] and Tuscany, curing these her sores which have already been long festering. Look how she prays God, that He send someone who might redeem her from these barbarous cruelties and insults; see also how she is ready and wholly disposed to follow a banner, provided there be one who takes it.

Nor is there anyone to be seen at present in whom she can hope more than in your illustrious House, which, with its fortune and virtue, favored by God and the Church (of which it is now the prince) could make itself the head of this redemption.[3] This will not be very difficult, if you[4] call up before you the actions and the lives of those named above.[5] And although these men are rare and marvelous, nevertheless they were men, and each of them had less occasion than that of the present; for their enterprise was not more just than this, nor easier, nor was God more a friend to them than to you. Here is great justice: "For just is the war for those for whom it is necessary, and pious the arms where there is no hope but in arms."[6] Here is the greatest of dispositions; nor can there be great difficulty where there is great disposition, provided that one takes, as a target, those orders which I have proposed.[7] Besides this, here are to be seen extraordinary things without example conducted by God: the sea has opened; a cloud has escorted you on the road; the rock has poured out water; here it has rained manna;[8] everything is concurring for your greatness. The rest ought to be done by you. God does not want to do everything, in order not to take away free will from us and that part of the glory which falls to us.

And it is nothing to marvel at if not one of the Italians named above has been able to do that which one can hope may be done by your illustrious House; and if, after so many revolutions in Italy and so much management of war, it always seems that military virtue is extinguished in her, this arises from her ancient orders not having been good. And there has since been no one who has known how to discover new ones; and nothing gives such honor to a man newly rising as the new laws and the new orders discovered by him. These things, when they are well founded and have greatness in them, make him revered and wonderful. And in Italy one does not lack matter for introducing every form; here there is great virtue in the members, were it not that she lacks heads. Look at the duels and combats which only involve a few, how the Italians are so superior in forces, skill and ingenuity. But when it comes to armies, they do not compare. And it all proceeds from the weakness of the heads; for those who know are not obeyed, and with everyone seeming to know, there has been no one until now who knew how to raise himself, through virtue and fortune, so that the others cede to him. From this it arises that so many times, in so many wars waged in the past twenty years, whenever there has been an army which was wholly Italian, it has always proved to be bad. Of this there is the testimony first of Taro,[9] and then Alessandria,[10] Capua,[11] Genoa,[12] Vailà,[13] Bologna,[14] Mestri.[15]

If, then, your illustrious House wishes to follow these excellent men[16] who redeemed their provinces, it is necessary, before all else, as the true foundation of every enterprise, to provide oneself with one's own arms; for one cannot have more faithful, or truer, or better soldiers. And although every one of them may be good, as one body they will become better when they see that they are commanded by their prince, and are honored and kept and provided for by him. It is necessary, therefore, to prepare for oneself these arms, so that with Italian virtue one can defend oneself against external powers.

And although the Swiss and Spanish infantry are esteemed as terrible, nevertheless both of them have defects, whereby a third order could not only oppose but be confident of surpassing them.[17]

For the Spanish are not able to withstand horse, and the Swiss have to fear infantry, when the latter are confronted in combat by men as obstinate as theirs. Whence one has seen and will see by experience that the Spanish are not able to withstand the French cavalry, and that the Swiss are routed by a Spanish infantry. And although the latter has not yet been fully confirmed by experience, yet an indication of it was seen in that day at Ravenna,[18] when the Spanish infantry were faced by German battalions, who follow the same order the Swiss do; where the Spanish, with their agile bodies and the aid of their bucklers, entered between and under their pikes, and safely attacked them without the Germans having any remedy; and if there had not been cavalry which charged [the Spanish], the latter would have annihilated all[of the Germans]. Knowing the defects of both these infantries, one can then order anew one which will resist horse, and which will not fear infantry: this will be done by the kind of arms [adopted] and by an alteration in orders.[19] And these are among those things which, newly ordered, give reputation and greatness to a new prince.

One ought not, then, let this occasion pass, so that Italy, after so much time, might see the one who is her redeemer. Nor can I express with what love he would be received in all those provinces which have suffered by these foreign floods; with what thirst for vengeance, with what obstinate faith, with what piety, with what tears. What doors would be shut against him? What peoples would deny him obedience? What envy would oppose him? What Italian would deny him homage? To everyone this barbarian domination stinks. Let your illustrious House, then, take up this task with that spirit and hope with which just enterprises are taken up; so that, beneath your ensign, this fatherland may be ennobled and, under your auspices, what Petrarch said may prove true:

> Virtue against the fury
> will take arms and make the battle short;
> for the ancient valor
> in Italian hearts is not yet dead.[20]

Notes

1. See Chapter VI, above.

2. It is commonly supposed that Machiavelli is referring to Cesare Borgia. But the description may apply to Machiavelli himself. See above, the Epistle Dedicatory; and *Discourses,* Epistle Dedicatory; I.Pref.; II. Pref. One should also take into account that Machiavelli finally indicates that Pope Alexander VI and not Cesare was the cause of the actions which are ostensibly praised. See Ch. XI, n. 8, above, and *Discourses,* III.29. See also n. 20, below.

3. Cardinal Giovanni de' Medici, uncle of the Lorenzo to whom *The Prince* is dedicated, had ascended to the papacy in 1513 as Pope Leo X. See Ch. XI, and the Epistle Dedicatory, n.4, above.

4. *recherete* — The courteous second person is used. Machiavelli returns to the formal address of the Epistle Dedicatory.

5. See Chs. VI and XIII, n. 13, above.

6. *iustum enim est bellum quibus necessarium, et pia arma ubi nulla nisi in armis spes est.* — Livy, *Histories,* IX.1.

7. See Ch. XIII, n. 15, above.

8. References to episodes in Exodus and Numbers, when God, as the "conductor" (see Ch. XII, n. 23, above) leads Moses and Israel towards the Promised Land. See also *Discourses,* II.8.

9. The River Taro, where the battle of Fornovo, July 5, 1495, was fought between the French and the Italians. Charles VIII was returning to France, in retreat from Naples. A blunder by the Italians prevented them from using their superior forces and permitted the French to escape.

10. Alessandria is a city in the Piedmont, lying across the western invasion routes. It was taken by Louis XII in 1499.

11. Capua was the last city of the Kingdom of Naples to hold out against the French. It was stormed and cruelly sacked by the French and Cesare Borgia in July, 1501.

12. The people of Genoa rebelled against French rule in 1507, overthrowing the oligarchy; it was immediately put down by Louis XII without difficulty.

13. See Ch. XII, n. 17, above.

14. The French chased Julius II out of Bologna, and restored the Bentivogli, May 21, 1511.

15. In 1513, a new war broke out with France and Venice on one side, and the Holy League (the Pope, the Emperor, Spain and Milan) on the other. Mestri was burned as the armies of the Holy League advanced on the Venetians.

16. See Ch. VI, n. 3; and Ch. XIII, n. 13, above.

17. Machiavelli treats of this point extensively in the *Art of War* (in Vol. II of the *Chief Works*), where he also speaks, in the Epistle Dedicatory of that work, of the error of dividing the civil life from military life. The middle way between the Swiss and Spanish infantry must of necessity be also a middle way with respect to *political* modes and orders. Since the Swiss are more ancient (Ch.X), and the Spanish are more modern, that is, Christian (Ch.XXI), one wonders what a middle way might be. See Strauss, *Thoughts on Machiavelli*, pp. 102, 172.

18. See Ch. XIII, n. 3, above.

19. *la variazione delli ordini* (an alteration in orders) — It must be emphasized that an alteration in orders is a change of the whole constitutional order or way of life. Most translators, however, seem to understand this phrase as having to do only with a change in battle tactics, methods, or formations. For the importance of the kind [*generazione*] of arms, see Ch. XIII, n. 8, above. The kind of arms one has, to repeat, is determined by one's modes — on which see the Introduction, Ch. I, n. 2; Ch. IV, n. 11; Ch. XVII, n. 15; and Ch. XXV, n. 3, above.

20.   *Virtù contro a furore*
    Prenderà l'arme; e fia el combatter corto:

Che l'antico valore
Nell 'italici cor non è ancor morto
—*Canzoniere* CXXVIII.93-96

Petrarch (1304-1374) wrote this *canzone* as an appeal "to the leaders of Italy" for unity against "the German fury." Foreign mercenaries commanded by the German Werner von Urslingen had led a campaign in Parma in the winter of 1344-45, a foretaste of what Italy was to suffer. (See the translation of *The Prince* by James B. Atkinson [Indianapolis: Bobbs-Merrill, 1976], p. 382 [n. 157]). In the *Florentine Histories,* VI.29, Machiavelli quotes a passage from another Petrarchean *canzone* (LIII), "Noble spirit which rules these limbs" (*Spirto gentil che quelle membra reggi*) when recounting the conspiracy of Stefano Porcari in Rome who "desired according to the custom of those men who have an appetite for glory, who do, or at least attempt, something worthy of memory; and he judged that he could attempt nothing other than to see if he could take his fatherland out of the hands of prelates and return her to the ancient life, hoping by this, when it would succeed, to be called a new founder and second father of that city." Machiavelli says that Stefano Porcari was above all given hope by the verses of Petrarch from *Spirto gentil,* which said:

On the Tarpeian mount, O Song, you will see
A knight whom all Italy honors,
More thoughtful is he of others than of himself.

(*Sopra il monte Tarpeio, canzon, vedrai*
Un cavalier che Italia tutta onora,
Pensoso più d'altrui che di se stesso.)

Machiavelli then comments that, "It was known to Messere Stefano that poets many times are full of the divine and prophetic spirit, so that he judged that in every mode those things which Petrarch had prophesied in that *canzone* would come to pass, and that he would be the one who would be the executor of so glorious an enterprise — since it seemed to him that by eloquence, by doctrine, by grace and by friends that he was superior to every other Roman. Having fallen then into this thought, he was unable to govern himself in so cautious a mode, that his words, his habits and his mode of life would not reveal him, such that he came to be suspected by the pontiff . . ."

As far as I have been able to discover, Machiavelli quotes passages from Petrarch three times in his works — at the end of *The Prince;* in Book VI.29 of the *Florentine Histories;* and at the end of the *Exhortation to Penitence* (in *Chief Works* I, pp. 171-174).

INDEX OF PROPER NAMES IN TEXT AND NOTES

(References are to chapters [Roman numerals] and pages.)

Achaeans III, 15; XIV, 89, 91 (n. 7); XXI, 133-4.

Achilles XIV, 90; XVIII, 107.

Acuto, Giovanni. See Hawkwood, John.

Aetolians III, 14, 15; XXI, 133.

Africa VIII, 52; XIX, 119; XXI, 133.

Agathocles the Sicilian VIII, 51-52, 54-55.

Agnadello. See Vailà.

Alba VI, 33.

Alberigo da Barbiano, Count of Conio. See Barbiano, Alberigo da.

Albinus   XIX, p. 117.

Alessandria XXVI, 153.

Alexander III the Great, of Macedonia IV, 25, 27; XIII, 84; XIV, 90; XVI, 98;
  XXIV, 144.

Alexander (Alexianus), Marcus Aurelius Severus, Emperor of Rome XIX, 115,
  116, 120.

Alexander VI, Pope (Rodrigo Borgia)   III, 17, 18, 19, 23 (n. 22); VII, 42-43,
  45, 46, 47; VIII, 53; XI 66, 67-68; XII, 76 (n. 5); XVIII, 108; XIX, 124
  (n. 10); XXVI, 155 (n. 2).

Alexandria XIX, 118.

Alexianus. See Alexander, Emperor of Rome.

Alfonso, King of Aragon XII, 73.

Amboise, Georges d'. See also Rouen, Cardinal of III, 19, 20 (n. 5), 24 (n. 26).

Angevins   XII, 77 (n. 10).

Antiochus II ("the Great") King of Syria   III, 15, 16; XXI, 133-134.

Antoninus Caracalla. See Caracalla.

Aquileia   XIX, 119.

Aragon   XII, 77 (n. 10).

Aragon, King of   XII, 73.

Ascanio.   See Sforza, Ascanio.

Asia   III, 22 (n. 7); IV, 25, 27; XIX, 117.

Athenians VI, 33; XXVI, 151.

Athens V, 29.

Baglioni.   See also Perugia   VII, 47.

Barbiano, Alberigo da, Count of Conio   XII, 75.

Bassianus, Varius Avitus.   See Heliogabalus.

Bentivoglio, Annibale   XIX, 113.

Bentivoglio, Giovanni. See also Bologna III, 17; XIX, 113; XXV, 148.

Bergamo, Bartolommeo da. See Colleoni, Bartolommeo da Bergamo.

Bologna, Bolognese VII, 43; XI, 68; XIII, 84-85 (n. 2); XIX, 113; XX, 129; XXV, 148; XXVI, 153.

Borgia, Cesare (Duke Valentino) III, 19, 23 (nn. 20, 22); VII, 42-48; VIII, 53-54; XI, 67-68; XIII, 82, 86 (n. 13); XVII, 100; XX, 129, 130; XXI, 136 (n. 1); XXVI, 155 (n. 2).

Borgia, Rodrigo. See Alexander VI, Pope.

Bracceschi XII, 73.

Braccio da Montone (Niccolò Fortebraccio) XII, 73, 75.

Brittany III, 12.

Burgundy III, 12.

Bussone, Francesco, Count of Carmignuola XII, 74.

Caesar (title) XIX, 117.

Caesar, Julius XIV, 90; XVI, 97, 98.

Caliphate, the XIX, 120; XXV, 149 (n. 2).

Camerino III, 17.

Canneschi, the XIX, 113.

Cantacuzene, John. See Constantinople, Emperor of

Capua V, 29; XXVI, 153.

Caracalla, Antoninus, Emperor of Rome XIX, 115, 116, 118, 120.

Caravaggio XII, 73.

Cardinals, College of VII, 46.

Carmignuola, Count of. See Bussone, Francesco.

Carthage V, 29.

Carthaginians VIII, 52; XII, 73.

Castile XXI, 132.

Caterina, Madonna. See Sforza, Caterina (Lady of Forlì).

Cesena VII, 45.

Charles VII, King of France XIII, 83-84.

Charles VIII, King of France III, 16, 20 (n. 5); XI, 67; XII, 72, 75.

Chiron the centaur XVIII, 107.

Christianity XIX, 121-124 (n. 6).

Christians XXI, 132.

Church, the, the Papacy III, 17-19, 23-24 (n. 23); VII, 42-43, 45-48; XI, 66-68; XII, 73, 74-75; XIX, 120, 124 (n. 10); XXI, 132, 135; XXVI, 152, 156 (n. 20).

Città di Castello XX, 129.

Colleoni, Bartolommeo da Bergamo XII, 74.

Colonna, the VII, 43, 44; XI, 67, 68.

Commodus, Marcus, Emperor of Rome XIX, 115, 116, 118-119, 120.

Conio, Alberigo da.   See Barbiano, Alberigo da.
Conio, Lodovico da.   See Barbiano, Alberigo da.
Constantinople, Emperor of   XIII, 82.
Cyrus the Great, King of the Medes   VI, 33, 34-35; XIII, 86-87 (n. 13); XIV, 90; XVI, 98; XXVI, 151.
Darius I, King of Persia   VII, 41.
Darius III, King of Persia   IV, 27.
David, King of Israel   XIII, 83.
Dido   XVII, 100.
Egypt   VI, 33; XXVI, 151.
Emperor, Holy Roman   X, 63; XII, 75; XXIII, 141.
Empire, Holy Roman   XII, 74-75.
English, the   XIII, 83.
Epaminondas   XII, 73.
Ercole d'Este, Duke of Ferrara   II, 8; III, 17.
Exodus.   See Old Testament.
Fabii, the   XVII, 105 (n. 12).
Fabius Maximus   XVII, 102.
Faenza   III, 17; VII, 43.
Ferdinand the Catholic (III of Aragon and V of Castile), King of Spain   I, 5; III, 17, 20 (n. 5); XII, 75; XIII, 81; XVI, 97; XVIII, 109; XXI, 132-133; XXV, 148.
Fermo. See also Oliverotto Euffreducci da Fermo   VIII, 53, 54.
Ferrara   II, 8; III, 17; XI, 67; XIII, 81.
Filippo, Duke.   See Visconti, Duke Filippo Maria.
Flamininus, Titus Quintius   XXIV, 144.
Florence, Florentines   III, 16, 20 (n. 5); V, 30; VI, 38 (n. 6); VII, 46; IX, 59; XI, 67; XII, 73-74; XIII, 82; XVII, 100; XIX, 113; XXI, 135.
Fogliani, Giovanni   VIII, 53-54.
Forlì   III, 17; XIII, 82.
Forlì, Lady of.   See Sforza, Caterina Riario.
Fortune XIV, 92 (n. 11); XX, 128; XXIV, 144; XXV, 146, 147, 149; XXVI, 152.
France, King of.   See also Charles VII, Louis XI, Louis XII   IV, 26.
France, Kingdom of, the French IV, 27; VII, 44, 46, 48; XI, 67, 68; XIII, 82, 83, 84; XIX, 114, 117; XXI, 133; XXV, 147; XXVI, 154.
Gaeta   VII, 45.
Gaius Sempronius Gracchus.   See Gracchi.
Gascony   III, 12.
Genoa   III, 16; XXVI, 153.

Germany, Germans   X, 63; XXV, 147; XXVI, 154.

Ghibellines   XII, 79 (n. 19); XX, 127.

Giovanna II, Queen of Naples   XII, 73.

Girolamo (of Forlì).   See Riario, Girolamo.

God   VI, 33; XII, 72; XXV, 146; XXVI, 152.

Goliath   XIII, 83.

Goths   XIII, 84.

Gracchi, the   IX, 59

Granada   XXI, 132.

Greece   III, 13, 14, 15, 16; IV, 27; V, 29; VII, 41; IX, 59; XIII, 82; XXI, 133; XXIV, 144.

Guelfs   IX, 61 (n. 6); XII, 79 (n. 19); XX, 127.

Hamilcar   VIII, 52.

Hannibal   XVII, 102.

Hawkwood, John (Giovanni Acuto)   XII, 73.

Hebrews   XXVI, 151.

Heliogabalus (Varius Avitus Bassianus) Emperor of Rome   XIX, 115, 119.

Hellespont, the   VII, 41.

Hiero II, tyrant of Syracuse   VI, 35; XIII, 83, 86-87 (n. 13).

Holy League, the   XII, 80 (n. 21); XIII, 84-85 (nn. 2-3).

Imola   XIII, 82.

Ionia   VII, 41.

Italy, Italians   II, 8; III, 12, 16, 17, 18, 19, 20-21 (n. 5); VII, 43; XI, 66-67; XII, 72, 74-75; XIII, 83; XIX, 117, 119; XXI, 133; XXIV, 143; XXV, 147; XXVI, 151, 152-153, 154, 156-158 (n. 20).

Joanna II.   See Giovanna II, Queen of Naples.

John VI Cantacuzene.   See Constantinople, Emperor of.

Julian, Marcus Didius, Emperor of Rome   XIX, 115, 117, 119.

Julius II, Pope (Giuliano della Rovere)   II, 8; VII, 47-48; XI, 68; XIII, 81; XVI, 97; XIX, 124 (n. 10); XXV, 148-149.

Leo X, Pope (Giovanni de' Medici)   Ep. Ded., 3 (n. 4); III, 23 (n. 23); XI, 68.

Liverotto.   See Oliverotto Euffreducci da Fermo.

Livy, Titus
   Histories   XXI, 134; XXVI, 152.

Locrians   XVII, 102.

Lombardy   III, 16, 17, 18, 19; XII, 73; XXI, 135; XXVI, 152.

Lorqua, Don Ramiro de.   See Orco, Remirro de.

Louis XI, King of France   XIII, 83.

Louis XII, King of France   III, 12, 16-19, 20-21 (n. 5); VII, 43, 45, 46; XII, 75; XXV, 148-149.

Lucca VII, 46.

Ludovico il Moro. See Sforza, Ludovico.

Macedonia. See also Alexander the Great, Philip III, Philip V III, 15.

Machiavelli XXVI, 155 (n. 2).

Macrinus, Marcus Opellius, Emperor of Rome XIX, 115, 119.

Magione VII, 44.

Mantua III, 17.

Marcus Aurelius the Philosopher, Emperor of Rome XIX, 115-116, 118, 120-121.

Marcus Commodus. See Commodus.

Marranos XXI, 132.

Maximilian I, Holy Roman Emperor XXIII, 141.

Maximinus, Caius Julius Verus, Emperor of Rome XIX, 115, 116, 119, 120.

Medes VI, 33; XXVI, 151.

Medici, Giovanni de'. See Leo X, Pope.

Medici, House of Ep. Ded., 3 (n. 4); XXVI, 152, 153, 154.

Mestri XXVI, 153.

Milan, Milanese. See also the Sforza, Visconti I, 5; III, 12, 17, 20-21 (n. 5); XII, 73, 76 (n. 9), 78 (n. 15); XX, 129-130.

Milan, Duke of. See also Sforza, Francesco VII, 42, 43; XI, 67; XII, 74; XXI, 135; XXIV, 143.

Montefeltro, Guido Ubaldo, Duke of Urbino XX, 129.

Moses VI, 33, 34-35; XIII, 86-87 (n. 13); XXVI, 151, 155 (n. 8).

Nabis, tyrant of Sparta IX, 59; XIX, 112.

Nantes III, 19.

Naples, King of. III, 17; XI, 67; XXIV, 143.

Naples, Kingdom of I, 5; III, 17, 18, 20 (n. 5); VII, 45, 46; XII, 73; XXI, 136 (n. 2); XXV, 148.

Niger. See Pescennius Niger.

Normandy III, 12.

Numantia V, 29.

Old Testament
  I Samuel XIII, 85 (n. 8).
  Exodus, Numbers XXVI, 155 (n. 8).

Oliverotto Euffreducci da Fermo VIII, 53-54.

Orco, Remirro de (Don Ramiro de Lorqua) VII, 45.

Orsini, the VII, 43, 44, 47; VIII, 54; XI, 67, 68; XIII, 82.

Orsini, Niccolò, Count of Pitigliano XII, 74.

Orsini, Paulo VII, 44.

Papacy, the. See Church, the.

Papal States   VII, 49 (n. 6); XI, 69 (n. 6).
Parliament (of France)   XIX, 114.
Persians   VI, 33; XXVI, 151.
Pertinax, Publius Helvius, Emperor of Rome   XIX, 115-116, 120.
Perugia   VII, 44, 46; XXV, 150 (n. 6).
Pescennius Niger   XIX, 117.
Petrarch
   Canzoniere XXVI, 154, 156-158 (n. 20).
Petrucci, Pandolfo   VII, 49 (n. 10); XX, 128; XXII, 138.
Philip II, King of Macedonia XII, 73; XIII, 84, 86-87 (n. 13).
Philip V, King of Macedonia   III, 15, 16; XXIV, 144.
Philopoemen of Megalopolis   IX, 61 (n. 4); XIV, 89-90.
Piombino   III, 17; VII, 46.
Pisa   III, 17; V, 30; VII, 46; XII, 74; XIII, 82; XX, 127.
Pistoia   XVII, 100; XX, 127.
Pitigliano.   See Orsini, Niccolò.
Pope, the.   See Church, the.
Porcari, Stefano   XXVI, 156-158 (n. 20).
Pyrrhus   IV, 28.
Ravenna   XII, 80 (n. 21); XIII, 81; XXVI, 154.
Remirro de Orco.   See Orco, Remirro de.
Riario, Caterina Sforza.   See Sforza, Caterina.
Riario, Girolamo (of Forlì)   XX, 130.
Riario, Raffaele, Cardinal of San Giorgio   VII, 48.
Rimini   III, 17, VII, 43.
Rinaldi, Luca   XXIII, 141.
Romagna   III, 17, 18, 19, 23 (n. 22); VII, 43, 44-45, 46, 47; XI, 68; XIII, 82;
   XVII, 100.
Roman Empire   XIII, 84; XIX, 119.
Roman Principate   I, 6 (n. 1); XVI, 97; XIX, 115, 118.
Romans   III, 14, 15-16; IV, 27; V, 29, 31 (n. 3); IX, 59; XII, 73; XIII, 84; XVII,
   102; XIX, 114-119, 120-121; XXI, 133-134; XXIV, 144; XXVI, 156-158
   (n. 20).
   in Greece: III, 22 (n. 13).
Rome VI, 33; VII, 46, 47; IX, 59; XI, 68; XII, 73; XIX 117, 118, 119; XXV, 149.
Romulus   VI, 33, 34-35; XIII, 86-87 (n. 13).
Rouen, Cardinal of (Georges d' Amboise)   III, 19, 20 (n. 5); VII, 48.
Rovere, Francesco della.   See Sixtus IV, Pope.
Rovere, Giuliano della.   See Julius II, Pope.
I Samuel, see Old Testament

Sangiachi   IV, 26.

San Giorgio, Cardinal.   See Riario, Raffaele.

San Severino, Roberto da   XII, 74.

Saul   XIII, 83.

Savonarola, Girolamo   VI, 34-35; XII, 76 (n. 6).

Scali, Giorgio   IX, 59.

Scipio Africanus Major, P. Cornelius   XIV, 90; XVII, 102-103.

Severus, Lucius Septimius, Emperor of Rome   XIX, 115, 117-118, 120-121.

Sforza, the   XII, 73, 75; XX, 129.

Sforza, Ascanio, Cardinal   VII, 48.

Sforza, Caterina (Lady of Forlì)   III, 17; XX, 130.

Sforza, Francesco   I, 7 (n. 6); VII, 42; XII, 73; XIV, 88; XX, 129.

Sforza, Giacomuzzo Attendolo   XII, 73.

Sforza, Ludovico, il Moro   III, 12.

Sicily   VIII, 52.

Siena   III, 17; VII, 46; XX, 128; XXII, 138.

Sinigaglia (Senigallia)   VII, 44; VIII, 54.

Sixtus IV, Pope (Francesco della Rovere)   II, 10 (n. 7); XI, 67.

Slavonia   XIX, 117.

Spain, Spaniards, Spanish.   See also Ferdinand the Catholic, (King of Spain) III, 18, 19; IV, 27; VII, 45-46, 48; XVII, 102; XXI, 132; XXV, 147, 148, 149 (n. 2); XXVI, 153-154.

Sparta, Spartans   V, 29; IX, 59; XII, 73.

Strauss, Leo
  on Walker's translation   I, 6 (n. 2).
  Thoughts on Machiavelli   III, 23 (n. 19); VI, 35-36 (n. 1); XV, 95 (n. 3); XVII, 105 (n. 12); XIX, 125 (n. 12); XXV, 149-150 (n. 3); XXVI, 156 (n. 17).

Sultan of Egypt   XIX, 120.

Swiss   X, 64-65 (n. 4); XII, 73, 75; XIII, 81, 83; XXV, 149-150 (n. 2), XXVI, 153-154.

Syracuse, Syracusans   VI, 35; VIII, 51-52; XIII, 83.

Tacitus   XIII, 86 (n. 12).

Taro (River)   XXVI, 153.

Thebes, Thebans   V, 29; XII, 73.

Theseus   VI, 33, 34-35; XXVI, 151.

Thrace   XIX, 119.

Tiberius Sempronius Gracchus.   See Gracchi.

Titus Quintius Flamininus.   See Flamininus.

Turk, the   III, 13; IV, 26, 27; XIX, 120.

ISBN 0-88133-444-8

9 780881 334449

90000